SCALEXTRIC COLLECTIBLES

Jonathan Mountfort

AMBERLEY

Highly detailed modern examples of classic 1960s F1 cars. Two Lotus 49 cars, one in the iconic red and gold 'Gold Leaf' livery, the other in British Racing Green. Alongside them is a blue Eagle Weslake.

First published 2018

Amberley Publishing
The Hill, Stroud
Gloucestershire, GL5 4EP

www.amberley-books.com

ISBN 978 1 4456 7909 9 (print)
ISBN 978 1 4456 7910 5 (ebook)

British Library Cataloguing in Publication Data.
A catalogue record for this book is available from the British Library.

Origination by Amberley Publishing.
Printed in the UK.

Contents

About the Book

First of all, what it is not: this book is not a catalogue of all the Scalextric items offered by the factory over the years, and neither is it a history of Scalextric – both of those subjects are covered in many other volumes, especially the excellent tomes written by Roger Gillham. What this book does do is to offer my personal view of starting a collection of the things (usually cars) that you would love to have and hold in your hand, either ones you already owned and lost, or others you never had but hankered after. Once you start collecting, almost all of the items you amass will be in the second category, for the whole thing is strangely addictive.

So here you will be able to read my tips for getting a collection you can be proud of and enjoy, for the budget that you can afford, although on this subject I must give a cautionary note: once the bug bites, you often spend more than you intended, and then go out and do it again a week later.

We shall look at and discuss the following:

- Finding out which are the bargains out there – even some of the really early cars are available in perfect condition in their boxes for not a lot of money.
- Deciding what you want to collect – this may be items from a period in Scalextric history, or a specific marque of car, or something else such as television and film related sets and vehicles. The choice is endless and yours to make.
- What to look out for when considering a purchase – unless customised on purpose, it is always best to go for cars that are as original as possible, with no modern reproduction parts and which have not been re-sprayed. However, customised cars are great fun and some are so meticulously and lovingly created that they are a joy to look at. Others, on the other hand, are just steampunk alien beasts. I have included many pictures of great variety.
- Cars that were offered as special limited editions at competitions, swapmeets, slot-car festivals and NSCC gatherings, plus 'range presentation' cars, which were handed out to dealers before the production version was released.

Returning to the subject of what this book is *not* about, there isn't the space to cover the plastic buildings that have been offered over the years. Besides, the cars are far more fascinating and are what most people enjoy collecting. However, the buildings are all described in Roger Gillham's 'Ultimate Guides' if you are interested.

The original trackside scenery of the early 1960s, made by the Young & Fogg Rubber Company Ltd of Wimbledon, South London, was all hand-painted, and because of its age is really quite fragile. Therefore some of these pieces are quite rare and hard to find in good condition. I have presented a selection of these attractive accessories, which included the huge (four-lane) Dunlop bridge modelled on the original at Le Mans with the clock tower on top, and also a photograph of the pair of Bridge Embankments (with their box), which is one of the rarest Scalextric items.

To make the pictures more varied and interesting, I asked Derek Duncombe of Scale Model Studio in Lincoln to handcraft some bridges and scenery specially for this book. You can see these in many of the photographs and, should you wish to purchase any of them for your own layout, contact scalemodelstudio via eBay.

Talking of eBay, obviously a lot of collecting takes place on that website and other similar ones on the internet. There are two things I would like to point out regarding sellers on these sites.

The first is that there appears to be a growing band of misguided vendors who seem to think that their Scalextric items are worth some kind of fortune, and offer a ridiculous 'Buy It Now' figure or equivalent starting bid. They presumably don't sell anything so my advice is just ignore them. A couple of years ago an excellent seller listed a lovely (just about perfect) Club 60 set with Austin Healey 3000 and Mercedes 190 with a Buy It Now price of £200. I was seriously tempted and my mouse finger hovered over the button, but I didn't press it, and neither did anyone else, for the listing ended unsold. The vendor relisted the set as an auction with a starting bid of 99p – it sold for £320!

The second thing is the word 'mint' and how it is bandied about willy-nilly on listings. 'Mint' means still in its box and unused, although an unboxed item can be described as mint if it is has been stored out of the dust and sunlight and is genuinely perfect. Sometimes you read 'fabulous car, totally mint, just missing one exhaust', which just about sums it up really. Ignore all the fine words and examine the photographs, assuming they are in focus and not taken through a mobile phone in a fog.

Above all, what I have tried to make this book about is conjuring up those memories of having fun!

Derek Duncombe at work in his scale model studio.

The Thrill and the Magic

I received my first (and only) Scalextric set for Christmas in 1964. It was a Formula Juniors set, with a figure-of-eight track with two 'Junior' cars – a blue Cooper and a red Lotus.

This was the cheapest set available at that time and, unsurprisingly, it still is ... you can pick up a nice one in good condition for around £30 to £40 today, which is much less than the equivalent price in real terms back then (£5 is around £200 today).

That was my only set, but of course, once I had a layout, I soon bought extra cars and track, the cost of which amounted to many weeks' pocket money, carefully saved. Many happy hours were spent with friends who brought their own track and cars round, giving us the challenge of setting out the largest circuit that the shape and size of the rooms in the house would allow. The hallway was long and thin, enabling the ideal Scalextric layout to be built, with two great long straights and as few corners as possible, for the cars were extremely fast even in those days, and much too fast for a twisty track. We always saved up to buy more and more straight sections so that the cars could be seen running at their full speed, our thumbs pressed down to the stops on the controllers for that briefest pleasure-filled moment before the next corner had to be negotiated.

I never bothered with Scalextric buildings, although plenty were available – it seemed a waste of money when I could buy a new car for the price of a couple of bits of static plastic that didn't do anything. The most important accessories were banking wedges to build the corners up to ridiculous angles in an attempt to keep the cars on the road at speed, and barriers to keep the back end of the car on the track when power sliding

The Formula Juniors figure-of-eight set with red Lotus and blue Cooper cars from 1964. Note the cardboard flyover supports printed with chequerboard, brickwork and SHELL banner – the first supports were just plain card, as shown later in the book.

round the bends. However, there was 'the spares rack'. My local shop where I bought all the things I could afford had a vertical wire rack with around a hundred different Scalextric spares bags hanging on it, and this was a wonderland. Now, it is perfectly logical that there would be things like packs of spare braids (the woven wire things that pick up the current from the track), spare guide pins, spare brushes (the brass and carbon things which deliver the current to the motor commutator), and spare tyres. I could even accept that every now and again I might need to buy a spare bumper (fender) for the front or back of a sports car, or a new windscreen (windshield). But there was all this other stuff… flags, axles, track clips, track-cleaning brushes, hedges, drivers, wiring harnesses – all small stuff and possibly useful – but then there were whole bodies for cars, and even motorcycles. The reason I remember the last two is because I could not afford to buy a vintage C65 Alfa Romeo (priced at £2 8*s* 11*d*, which is £2.45 in decimal but, more to the point, around £100 in today's value). I saw the blue body in its spares bag priced at around 5*s*, and next to it another bag with the underpan. There were bags nearby with the axles and wheels, another supplied the wiring harness, and the RX motor used in almost all the cars was easy to find. Round guide pins were only a couple of pence. I gathered up the whole lot and totted up the price – it came to less than half that of buying the complete car! I was missing the driver, but that didn't matter, I had a car that worked and the fun of putting all the bits together. A few weeks later I repeated the process with a B1 Typhoon motorcycle (list price £1 9*s* 6*d*, almost £1.50 in decimal, but now it would be £60). I think those two 'bitsas' gave me more fun than all the other cars I owned – it was as if I had designed and built them myself!

But nothing lasts forever, and after a few years of use the battered cars and accessories were retired to the attic where many thousands around the world still reside to this day. Had the magic ended? Not really – we just discovered other toys and pastimes until many, many years later, surrounded by the beeps and shrieks of computer games, we wondered what it would be like to be able to play with a proper toy again, like we did when we were the correct age for such a thing. We now look on the internet and find there is still lots to choose from, from whatever era we enjoyed, so we buy our first piece of memorabilia, usually a car, pick up some second-hand track and a transformer (or buy some modern track – it works just as well, and probably better) and off we go! The thrill and the magic is back…

The excitement of carrying home a small brown paper bag containing vital spares like these round guides from the 1960s, which were found still in the bag in 2018, never leaves you.

Starting Out – What You Can Get For Not a Lot

No matter what Scalextric era you wish to collect, there are some beautiful cars to be had for not a lot of money. Here is a selection so you know what to look for.

1960s

When Tri-ang took over the Scalextric brand in 1960, it produced the first plastic cars, initially just four in number: the Vanwall and front-engined Lotus Formula One cars, and the Lister Jaguar and Aston Martin sports cars. These cars were initially fitted with what are known as 'loop-braids', which wear out fairly quickly because the area of contact with the track is always in the same part of the braid and cannot be adjusted. Loop-braid cars are out of fashion at the time of writing this book and so can be picked up, often in their boxes, for very reasonable sums. Versions with head and taillights were made in the second year and these can be found very easily too.

Almost all the cars were also made in a factory in Calais and these French cars can be fun to collect, some coming in different colours never used by the English factory at Havant.

The second generation of plastic cars has a 'round guide' where the front of the car rides on the ends of the braids, so as they wear they just get shorter and can be adjusted to feed more braid through from the inside.

One of the first four plastic cars, the Lister Jaguar, with loop-braids and 'big head' driver. Note that this car has spent some time skidding along on its driver's head –the paint is worn off the top of the helmet. Expect to pay £30 to £40 for a boxed one with no brown marks on the bodywork, as in the picture. The box has the correct yellow colour spot to match the car.

Scalextric was an expensive toy in the early 1960s. In 1963 Tri-ang produced a budget range of cars called ' Formula Juniors', which have smaller motors, steerable front wheels and no proper braids, just pieces of wire. These cars were around half the price of a standard car – 15*s* 11*d* (80p) against 29*s* 6*d* (£1.50). Most of these are still relatively inexpensive now, although there are rare ones for the collector to seek out.

Motorcycles became available early on, or to be exact, motorcycle combinations. These are belt driven by a transverse motor to very thin wheels with unbelievably narrow tyres and great skill is required to keep them from tipping over or spinning round on the track.

The famous Mini arrived in Scalextric form in 1965. It is powered by a Juniors motor fitted back to front, giving front-wheel-drive like the real car, but the front wheels don't steer (which is a problem with front-wheel-drive) and the current collection is also problematic. Unfortunately, it didn't work too well and was soon replaced with a rear-wheel-drive version. However, they were made in large numbers and are readily available, and are actually a very nice model, and fun to get working if you have the patience.

The later version of the Lister Jaguar (green car) has a round guide and a smaller driver's head. The car in the picture is the lighted version and has the two characteristic dark marks at the front caused by gas given off from the rubber bulb holders and heat from the lamps. The red car is a D-type Jaguar and the yellow car is the Porsche Spyder. Expect to pay £40 to £50 for each of these in their boxes.

The English Cooper and Lotus Juniors can be found in beautiful condition for £15 to £20 each – and they come in a range of colours. The yellow Lotus in the picture above is a French Junior made in the Calais factory. Expect to pay £10 more for a French car like this one, but considerably more for rare colours. Note that the racing number is in a different, narrower font than the British ones.

The Typhoon motorcycle combination, seen here surmounting the rubber hump back bridge with hand-painted walls made by Young & Fogg, can be bought for around £40 to £50 with nice unblemished paintwork.

The front-wheel-drive Mini, like the red one above, can be bought very cheaply for around £20 without a box – make sure it has its little black plastic cover over the gear wheel on the front axle. The Triumph TR4 will be at least £60 if it has its original windscreen intact and faded chrome bumpers. Beware shiny ones – they are usually reproduction.

1970s

Tri-ang were in financial trouble at the start of the 1970s and Scalextric was sold off to Dunbee-Combex-Marx. The range of cars and accessories was reduced substantially to cut costs and production was moved from Havant in Hampshire to the Rovex factory in Margate, hence the Rovex name appearing on all the literature from this time. The Tri-ang Scalextric operation had run into trouble mainly because of two products: You Steer, in which the cars move from side to side on the track using a wheel on the hand controller, and Super 124, which was larger scale, aimed at the slot car club market, and extremely expensive. The new owners quickly dropped these lines and concentrated on the normal cars that people loved. One of the stars of the '70s was the 'power sledge'.

Some '70s cars are just a shell with a motor, like the Lamborghini Miura, and sold in vast quantities. These are very common and easy to find.

When the Ford Escort arrived in the 1970s, it was very nicely modelled and soon became available as several lighted versions.

Many French cars in the '70s were of their own design and were never manufactured in England, but some were available in the English catalogue and were imported from across the Channel.

The Calais factory was actually owned by Tri-ang. When they wanted to set up a similar facility in Spain, it was more difficult because of the dictatorship of General Franco. The Spanish Exin firm were given a licence to use the Scalextric name and produce their own models of car to sell as Scalextric.

The Lotus Indianapolis 'Power Sledge' car. The bodies of these cars just clip onto the back axle of the Power Sledge chassis, which can actually be run on its own without a body at all. These were the fastest things around until Magnatraction arrived in 1988, and are much more fun to drive because the tails slide around. You can get a Lotus like this one for around £40 in good condition, and the red Ferrari is similar in price. The first Power Sledge cars, the Panther and Europa Vee, can be had for even less.

The Lamborghini Miura is a very common car from the 1970s and sells for £15 to £20 for the Hong Kong, English or USSR version.

Above: Mk 1 Ford Escort Mexico Special Builds with racing stripe livery cost around £20 each.

Right: If you would like to start collecting cars made in the Calais factory, the French produced a budget range in flip-top boxes like the one shown above. The Alfa Romeo is one of the nicest and can be had for around £30, although the example shown on the right is losing a little paint from its rear wing.

Spanish cars are more expensive but are beautifully made and of much higher quality than the English and French cars of the time. The Porsche, although looking modern, has the RX motor, which was fitted to all the early Tri-ang cars and so was probably made in the 1970s. This mint unused boxed example cost £40. The iconic six-wheel P34 Tyrrell Formula 1 car was never listed in the UK catalogues. It is a masterpiece of model engineering and well worth around £80 in a nice Spanish box.

1980s

Dunbee-Combex-Marx also ran into financial trouble at the start of the 1980s and Scalextric was bought out by Hornby, makers of the model railways and train sets, becoming Hornby Hobbies. Thankfully they are still the owners at the present time.

360 degree racing arrived in the '80s with the rotating guide blade enabling the cars to spin around and travel in either direction.

The yellow Renault RS-01 (top left) was the first turbocharged car in Formula 1. The six-wheel March (top right) never ran in a Grand Prix race but looked interesting enough for Scalextric to make a model. Bottom left and right are the Tyrrell 008 and Ferrari 312 T3. All these cars mint in their boxes can be bought for around £25 to £30 each. An interesting fact: all the RS-01 Renaults are stamped 'RS-03' on the base.

Cars with 360 degree fully rotating guides arrived in the shape of 'Super Stox' based on stock cars and 'Mini Banger Racers' named *Mad Hatter* and *Mini Ha-Ha*. Mint in box these should cost around £40 to £50 each.

1990s

Batman and The Joker arrived in the 1990s and the cars, illustrated above as they crash across the 'Flying Leap' (included in the 'Batman Leap' set), will cost around £20 for a mint boxed Joker Porsche and £30 for a Batmobile.

2000s

Five IndyCar Dallaras in assorted colourful liveries – all five mint unused in their boxes only cost the author £66, including postage!

2010s

Two modern cars (Bugatti Veyron and BMW Mini) and a go-kart, all mint and unused for less than £20 each. The go-kart is double the scale of the cars, as can be seen by the size of its driver compared with the spectator figures.

What To Look Out For

So you loved your Scalextric set as a kid and now you would like to hold those beautiful cars in your hand again, but not the bashed up ones with half a wing and one wheel and the driver's head missing. The first piece of advice is: always buy the best you can within your budget.

Some people enjoy fixing wrecks, and that's fine and they are to be admired. If you are into customising then quite often a wreck is exactly what is needed. But it's strange that nowadays sometimes the price someone will pay for a wreck is not much lower than for a really good original example of the same car – so just buy a nice one in the first place, and if it has a box then so much the better. The only problem with this approach is that you're afraid of breaking it, so you put it on the track to race and either trundle round, being careful, and get whipped by your children, or you get carried away, hit the throttle, fly off the bend and smash that fifty-year-old chrome bumper (I know – I have done this!). If you want to race the old cars then perhaps get ones that are minus their bumpers already, or remove them if that's possible before you launch them on the track. The original vintage cars from the 1960s – the blower Bentley and the Alfa Romeo – actually advised the user on the instruction leaflet to remove the mudguards before racing them. This was fine with the Alfa as without its mudguards it was pretty unbreakable, but the Bentley has a chrome fishtail exhaust pipe and this always got snapped off.

The solution then: buy one perfect one and one to race. And on the subject of racing old slot cars, the original tyres do not work after fifty years, but modern replacements are now available for all the old cars and they stick like glue – fitted with these they actually go faster than they did when fresh out of the box.

What Theme Would You Like?

You may choose a theme, or you may just fall into one after you've bought your first few cars. Once you hold them, you'll know which ones you like best.

There are themes by function: police cars, or track marshal cars, or Grand Prix cars, or rally cars, or motorcycles.

There are themes by make of car: just Ferraris, or Porsches, or...

There are themes by era: early cars from the '60s, or even earlier tinplate cars (not many to choose from), or cars from this century.

There are themes by club or event: Scalextric Club cars, National Scalextric Collectors' Club (NSCC) cars, Dutch Collectors' Club (SLN) cars, Slot Car Festival cars, swapmeet cars etc., etc.

There are themes by country of manufacture: Made in… England, France, Spain, Mexico, Hong Kong, Australia/New Zealand, USSR, and a few more.

Or you could just collect Ford Escorts, or Minis – there are hundreds of them…

And there is always the popular television and film theme.

A Quick Guide to Guides

The guide is the fundamental functioning item on a slot car – it picks up current to make the car go and follows the slot to steer the car around the track. The evolution of the guide to the one we use today was remarkably quick – just seven years from the 'gimbal' of the tinplate cars to the pivoted blade, which hasn't changed in the last fifty years. Below is a quick guide.

The 'gimbal' guide on the 1950s tinplate cars did two jobs in one: it both picked up the current and followed the slot in the track. Its main drawback was that it was too free-running. When you let go of the trigger on the controller with a modern car, it slows down very quickly, enabling it to take a sharp bend. After releasing the power button on the tinplate cars, they keep rolling for a long time, so cornering is very tricky.

The first plastic cars had what is known as a 'loop-braid'. This is because the woven wire that picks up the current is attached at both ends, as shown in the picture. The functions of current collection and guiding were now separated, a single narrow nylon pin following the slot and steering the car. The drawback of the loop-braid is that it always uses the same contact patch on the braid so it wears out very quickly – this can be seen in a later picture.

The loop-braid very quickly changed to the second generation 'round guide'. This clamps a straight piece of braid in any position, so when the ends in contact with the rails wear down, it is an easy job to feed an extra length through the slits in the guide. It also has the advantage that the length of braid can be adjusted to give the ideal ride height for the pin in the track slot.

When the cheap Juniors cars were launched in 1963, they had a moving guide that steered the front wheels. However, there were no braids, just two bent copper wires.

When Scalextric produced the first model of the Mini in 1965, they followed the prototype by making it front-wheel-drive. This was awkward as it meant the electrical pick-up and the driving wheels were at the same end of the car, and both needed to have good contact with the track. The attempt at a solution was to mount the guide and braids on two long copper strips – these can be seen in the picture running all the way from the two screws at the left to the guide at the right. This enabled the braids to bounce up and down, following the conductor rails, but it never worked satisfactorily and the Scalextric Mini soon became rear-wheel-drive.

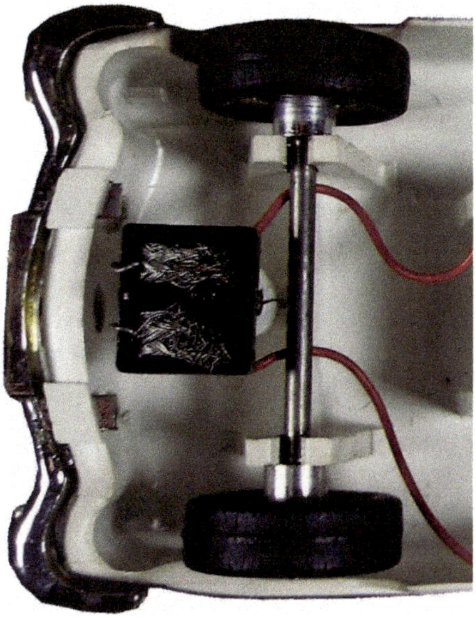

Above left: The Mercedes 190 and Austin Healey cars had a guide mounted on a post moulded into the car. This made it very easy to change the guide, but the post was easily cracked, as shown in the picture above. This is a very common fault on these cars.

Above right: The arrival of the pivoted 'blade guide' in 1966 signalled the end of the evolution of the design. This shark-nose Ferrari has a blade guide whose general form has not changed other than cosmetically in the succeeding fifty years.

Above left: The Spanish cars have a blade guide of their own shape and colour.

Above right: The modern blade guide clicks into place and so is more easily exchanged for a new one, but its general form is no different from that of 1966.

Return of the loop-braid! The 360 degree rotating guides for cars that can spin right round and run in either direction are pretty much the loop-braid of 1961, but they are longer and flatter and so don't wear out as quickly.

Boxes

Not only is it nice to have a good original box for a car, it will also (usually) have kept the contents in better condition over the years, although of course this will depend on where it has been stored for all this time. A box will always add value to a car, though often not a great amount, but it is still worth seeking out boxed examples for your collection if you can find them. A rare box may double the price, but this is highly unusual. Each section of the book discusses the early boxes for the country that made them – these being Britain, France and Spain. Later boxes are almost all hard see-through plastic and are not covered here. The French used this type of box very early on, as seen in the picture of the Alfa Romeo shown previously.

Brown Marks

You will see that many of the early plastic cars have brown marks, usually over the wheel arches. These are especially visible on the lighter colours such as yellow or white. The most common cause is the tyres themselves. The rubber gives off a gas (which is the rubber smell) and over the years this reacts with the plastic, turning it brown. The warmer the conditions the car is kept in, then the more gas there is given off. For this reason, try and store cars in a cool dry place. Also, if you have a perfect one with no brown marks, store it with the tyres removed. Another cause of brown marks is the heat from lamps on lighted cars – see the example in the pictures shown here.

Take note: a car with no brown marks can be worth twice as much as one with even faint signs of having them.

This French Aston Martin from the early 1960s shows the common brown marks which these cars experience, especially the lighted cars like the one pictured, and they are most noticeable against the yellow colour.

This is the base of the same car, showing the brown marks where the rubber mountings for the lighting poke through the bodywork.

Warped Bodywork

Another very common problem with old plastic cars is warping of one or both halves of the bodywork so the two pieces no longer mate properly and there is a gap along the sides. Some cars are more prone to this than others – D-type Jaguars from the '60s seem to have this happen a lot, and the Super 124 E-type Jaguars are particularly bad. It also depends on the quality of plastic used – Spanish cars don't warp, but the exact same car made in Mexico is often twisted out of shape. When you are buying old cars, check to see how well the sides join at the seam. Sometimes (experience with the D-type Jaguar again) the warping is so bad that the rear axle is too stiff for the motor to turn.

This picture shows a very common fault with older plastic cars where the two halves of the body have warped slightly and no longer fit snuggly together. This picture also shows how the original loop-braids wear out quickly at the point where they touch the metal rails on the track.

Mould

You have a nice car, in its box, and store it away for a couple of years in the attic maybe, or a quality garden shed or cabin. You eventually decide to look at your collection, maybe to show it off to a friend, and on opening the box the car, which was pristine and shiny, is covered in a white powdery substance – and it's everywhere: all over the body, the base, under the windscreen, and inside around the motor and axles. This is caused by a slight dampness during storage – and it doesn't take much either; the damp may not even be noticeable. Even the tyres can get the dreaded mould.

Many people have many different methods of getting rid of this stuff. Here it is just recommended that you take a used dry toothbrush and gently scrub it away, being careful not to damage any paintwork or stickers or decals, or snap off any bumpers or headlights. Take your time and have patience.

For really bad cases of mould that won't come off with a toothbrush there are many suggested methods of removing it, which can be found by doing a search on the internet.

For tyres covered in mould, remove them, then soak them in olive oil overnight. Clean them with a dry cloth the next day, and not only will the mould have gone, but they will be soft and supple once more and will grip the track better.

Another common problem with the old plastic cars is white mould growing on the plastic, probably caused by slight dampness – and it doesn't have to be very damp at all! Unless it is really bad, this can be removed by gently brushing with an old dry toothbrush.

Just five minutes with the dry toothbrush and the mould is gone from the Typhoon motorcycle. Note that the paintwork was already worn off in places and is not any worse after brushing. Remember to split the body and do the inside as well.

The Re-Spray and the Repro

Most sellers are honest and tell you if a car has any reproduction parts or has been sprayed a different colour. But here are just a few tips to show what to look for when buying, to make sure that all is as it should be. Of course there is nothing wrong with buying cars that have been refurbished or have had a change of colour, as long as you know this when you buy and don't pay as much as you would for an unmolested one.

For spotting the re-spray, the first thing to note is the patina of the finish on the bodywork. Old cars look old – even perfect ones. The tone of the colour will vary a tiny amount, especially around the edges of wheel arches. We mentioned brown marks in an earlier section – if an old car has even the faintest brown tinge around the wheel arch, or on the tips of the mudguards on, say, a French yellow Alfa Romeo, then it definitely hasn't been re-sprayed.

A painted car may well smell different from an unpainted one– we all know what one of the early plastic cars should smell like: even after many years the fragrance does not go away. Cars from Spain smell different from the English and French ones – slightly sharper – and the Mexican ones even more so. Spanish STS sets (*see page 59*) have a really strong overpowering odour all of their own. Looking inside the car may show patches of the original colour that has not been properly covered, especially where the back axle bearings push into the plastic mounts on the base.

Reproduction parts, especially chrome-work such as bumpers and exhausts, are usually given away by their shininess – some original chrome on early cars does stay very shiny, but more often it has a faded, aged quality that confirms its years. If it is possible to open the car up, it is easier to spot reproduction chrome as it is normally glued into place, whereas the originals are melted in, as shown in the pictures.

Original bumpers on an Aston Martin DB4. See how the plastic mounting posts have been melted and are spread over the bumpers, showing that they have never been removed.

Shark-nose Ferrari exhausts break very, very easily and so are fitted with reproduction ones more often than not. The originals shown on the left are clear inside the chrome plating and are melted over the bodywork. The original exhausts can also be spotted because they will have a dull chrome patina on the tailpipes. The repro ones on the right are very shiny and the mounting pins will be pushed into place and glued. The green shark nose is unusual in that it has been converted to a 'can' motor instead of the usual RX motor as fitted to the red one.

Interiors/Driver Platforms

There are many combinations of interior and exterior colours and, as one would expect, some combinations are rare and therefore more collectible.

Racing Number Roundels

Racing numbers will often be missing, or will have modern replacements as they are very fragile and fall off easily when the original glue hardens. Old numbers will look old – usually with brown tinges and frayed edges. French numbers often (but not always) used a different, narrower font than the English ones, as can be seen in the picture.

Almost all Ferrari 250s and Aston Martin DB4s were fitted with interior mouldings of seats etc. (driver platforms) that were a different colour from the bodywork. This French Ferrari 250 has a blue interior fitted to a blue car and is quite rare – this feature probably doubles the price you'd pay for one of these.

A French Aston Martin DB4 with its original racing number roundel. You can tell it is original because it looks browned and old, but also the number is in a very narrow font, which is only used by the French factory in Calais. The number 5 Ferrari in the previous picture has had replacement self-adhesive numbers fitted at some time.

Code 3 Models vs. Custom

A model that is a standard factory issue, and which is then subsequently redecorated in different livery, transfers, tampo print, colour etc., is known as a 'Code 3'. This is different from a fully customised car, wherein the basic shell is taken and the whole thing is remodelled with parts added or removed, and bits from two or three other models are often combined to produce something that no longer looks like the base car. Over the years, the factory has produced many cars with a version in a plain white finish with no decoration so that Code 3 modellers can easily finish them in any livery they desire.

Swapmeets, Toy Fairs and Collectors' Clubs

Before the advent of internet shopping, collectors attended swapmeets and toy fairs to meet knowledgeable people who share the same interests, and to try and track down any models that they required for their collection. These events still take place and are a good source of both knowledge and desirable items, but obviously the online sites now enable anyone to search for anything and usually it will be available, although without the advantage of being able to inspect and examine it 'in the flesh'. For this reason, swapmeets and toy fairs are still useful to hold and feel the actual object you might wish to purchase.

Collectors' clubs fall into two categories: the ones run by the manufacturer, in this case the Scalextric Club (which usually produces one or two models a year that can only be purchased if you are a member, although they soon appear on sites such as eBay once released); and clubs run by groups of enthusiasts, such as the British NSCC (National Scalextric Collectors' Club), Dutch SLN (Scalextric Liefhebbers Nederland) and ASRCC (Australian Scalextric Racing and Collecting Club), plus numerous other smaller ones and others in different countries. These clubs will often commission their own cars from the manufacturer, or from a Code 3 supplier, and many of these are illustrated in this book.

Morris Mini police car in HEDDLU Dyfed-Powys Constabulary livery, one of a hundred specially made for the Swindon Swapmeet, 4 January 2015.

The Tinplate Years

Fred Francis was an engineer and toolmaker who after the Second World War began manufacturing tinplate toy cars with 'pull-back' clockwork motors – you put the car on the floor, you pull it back, you let it go, and off it zooms… His company was called Minimodels and he gave these cars the brand name 'Scalex'. In the mid-1950s he had the idea of putting an electric motor into a Scalex car and called these Scalextric – a *Scalex* car which is elec*tric*. The track with a slot down the middle to guide the cars had been experimented with before by German and British inventors, but it was Scalextric that became the brand name known around the world, and it was Scalextric that was the first slot car system that was commercially successful.

The initial tinplate cars chosen for electrification were the Formula One Maserati and Ferrari of the time, and later the Austin Healey sports car. An early catalogue also shows a Jaguar and an Aston Martin DB2 from the Scalex range, but neither of these was ever released as a Scalextric car.

From its little factory in Havant, Hants, Minimodels produced a few electric Maseratis, put two of them in a box, and announced the toy at the Harrogate International toy fair in January 1957 – orders were then taken for set No. 1 with two Maseratis.

After a few months the Ferrari was ready and sets Nos 2 and 3 were launched, each with one of each make of car, set No. 3 having a flyover figure-of-eight track layout.

A lovely Minimodels drawing of the tinplate Scalextric car. The motor is mounted transversely at the rear of the car, driving the back axle via a plain spur gear. Only one rear wheel had a rubber tyre, so the car was effectively single-wheel-drive to make cornering easier. The gimbal pick-up (called a swivel in the text) has just one wire to the motor, the other feed being via the tin chassis.

The Austin Healey was not ready until much later – possibly after the takeover by Tri-ang, which happened in November 1958. For a few years Tri-ang continued with the tinplate cars until the first plastic ones were ready for sale in 1960.

Set No. 1. Two Maserati cars, as driven by Juan Manuel Fangio at the time and thus the state-of-the-art in Grand Prix racing. The track is made of rubber. The controller (top left) is shared by the two drivers and each has a simple push-button, on or off. Top right is the battery box, although the whole thing worked much better with a model railway transformer. This set still has its cardboard cut-out cover over the components – stunningly rare to see as most were discarded. Note that the Scalextric sign in the centre has Tri-ang underneath, so this is a late set No. 1 after Tri-ang had taken over the Scalextric brand. They added the cover to get their name on the set without having to reprint the box artwork.

Set No. 2. One Maserati and one Ferrari (in blue). Strangely, although many Scalex Ferraris were sprayed up in red, none of the Scalextric ones were. The trackside fencing in these early sets is much nicer than the later cheap and nasty white barriers introduced by Tri-ang.

Two Maseratis and a Ferrari pass the pits at speed, their rubber drivers staring ahead in concentration.

The 1950s Maserati with the modern tinplate reissue of the same car in the foreground. Assuming the new car is 1/32 scale, this shows that the old car is more like 1/28 or even bigger.

Tri-ang Bag a Winner

With Tri-ang's worldwide reputation and marketing machine, Scalextric hit the big time and began to sell in large quantities, especially from 1960, when the lighter and more nimble plastic cars arrived, along with the variable speed hand controller, which made a huge improvement to the enjoyment of the game. The track was initially still of the fairly stiff rubber variety, but this was soon changed to plastic 'Plexytrack', which was very flexible and could accommodate being raised at one side into very high banking so the cars would stay in the slot at high speeds around the corners. This was exciting stuff as scale speeds of 150 mph were now perfectly feasible.

The first plastic cars have model numbers starting with C (for Car): C/54 Front Engine Lotus Formula One car, C/55 Vanwall Formula One car, C/56 Lister Jaguar Competition car, and C/57 Aston Martin Competition car. Why the numbering started at 54 is a mystery. Later on the numbers lower than 54 were used, with C/1 ending up as a Renault Alpine made in France!

The first form of pick-up used on the plastic cars is what is now known as the 'loop-braid'. As pointed out earlier, loop-braid cars are out of fashion and can be purchased for very reasonable prices.

The working parts of a loop-braid car. Early plastic cars such as this Porsche Spyder have a metal crown gear (sometimes called a contrate gear) which drives the rear axle. The motor is an RX, which was the same motor as was fitted to Tri-ang model trains at the time. In front of the RX motor is the housing for the loop-braid guide along with a suppressor to reduce sparking, and hence radio and TV interference. The front axle has a cloth tube place in the centre to make locating the axle in its mounts easier. This was soon done away with and nearly all cars just have the brass bushes, which can be seen at each end of the axle. The Porsche Spyder in loop-braid form is rare as nearly all had the later round guide.

In the second catalogue under Tri-ang ownership it was announced that the Lister Jaguar and Aston Martin sports cars would be available with working lights. Night-time Scalextric racing became possible, with head and taillights zooming round an almost completely invisible track.

After a short time the troublesome loop-braid was replaced with the second generation round guide with the familiar adjustable braids. The metal crown gear drive to the back axle was replaced with a plastic one.

The Aston Martin DB4 and Ferrari 250 Grand Touring cars were also fitted with lights, along with a black version of the DB4 decorated with MARSHAL transfers and with a working roof light. The five lighted cars had model numbers beginning with

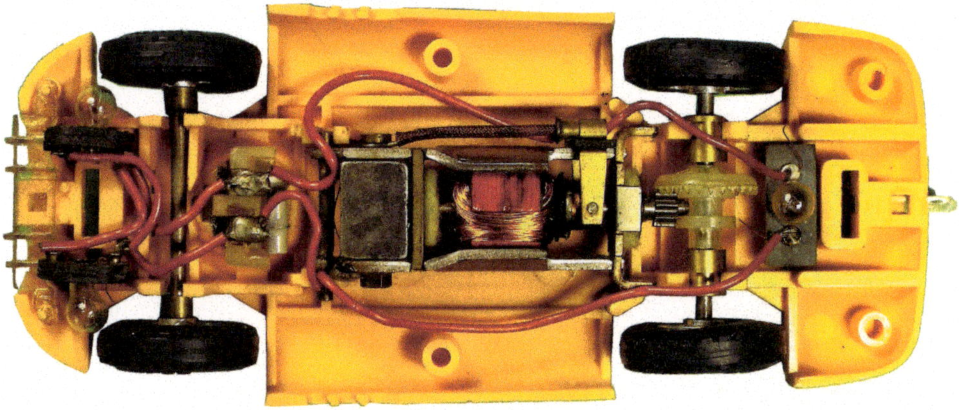

Here is the inside of the French Aston Martin with lights, as shown earlier. This car, along with the Lister Jaguar, was the first to be fitted with lights and the wiring layout can be seen clearly in the picture. The French version shown has the more curvaceous rounded bulbs for the lighting, while the English ones are capsule shaped, with the same diameter all the way along the glass envelope. The French RX motor windings are brighter and more orange coloured.

The later Porsche Spyder with round guide and plastic crown gear (contrate). The Porsche in its original form was very tail-happy because it has a very short wheelbase and was too light at the back, so Scalextric fitted a metal weight, which improved its handling tenfold. Note that the white mould is starting to creep in at the front – easily removed with the dry toothbrush.

E (for Electric lights): E/1 Lister Jaguar Competition car, E/2 Aston Martin Competition car, E/3 Aston Martin DB4 Grand Touring, E/4 Ferrari 250 Grand Touring, and E/5 Aston Martin Marshal's car.

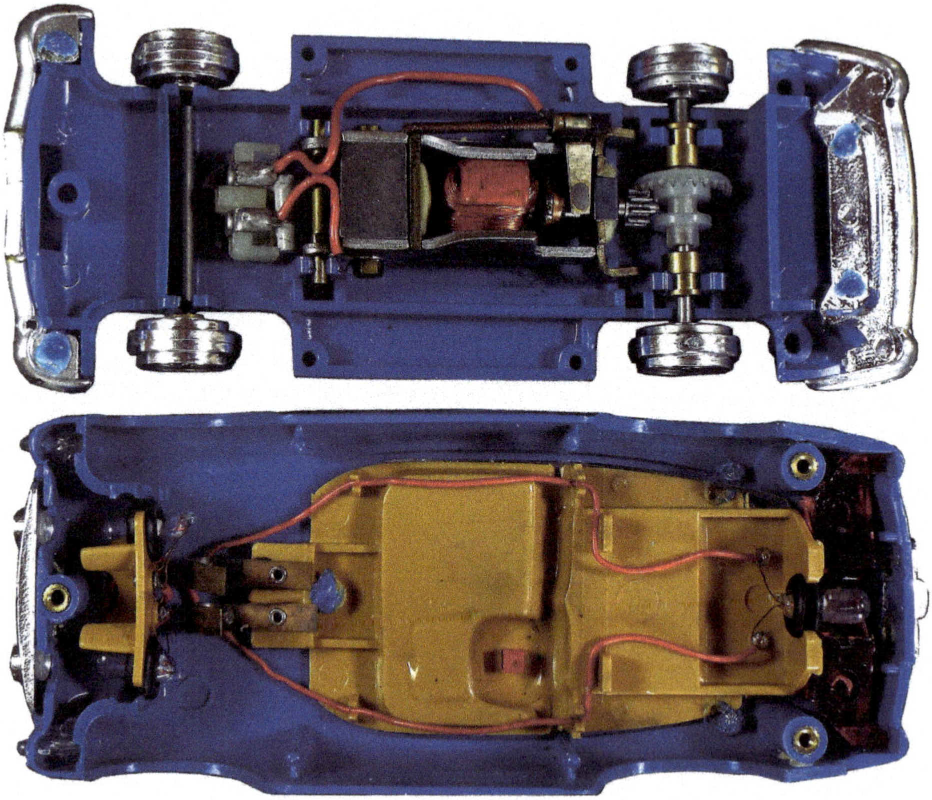

The lighting in the Ferrari 250 and Aston Martin DB4 cars (DB4 shown here) is fitted to the top half of the body and contacts via brass strips pressing against the soldered joints of the guide.

Young & Fogg

The Young & Fogg Rubber Co. Ltd, based in Wimbledon SW19 (south-west London), manufactured balloons and other rubber novelties and toys trading under the name Gartex. They became part of Tri-ang in around 1958/59 and from that time produced a whole range of trackside accessories and buildings for both the model railways and Scalextric.

Pictured here are the main items produced by Young & Fogg that featured in the Scalextric catalogues from the early 1960s.

1955 advertising: 'It is super-quality, the "Gartex" range! The bright, floating balloons, the toys, dolls and ingenious novelties are in delightful designs, made from the finest quality, long-lasting rubber. Their gay colours are protected by a finish that is fast and hygienic, making them the most acceptable of toys.'

The rubber humpback bridge sides made and hand-painted by Young & Fogg Rubber Company. Did Young & Fogg also make the rubber drivers for the tinplate cars?

A round guide BRM being refuelled on the rubber humpback bridge in the snow.

The rubber Dunlop bridge complete with clock à la 'Le Mans'. Two Ferrari 250s are shown – the common red version, and the rare French yellow at ten times the price. Note that the Ferrari does not have its tyres fitted as it has been stored without them to avoid brown marks, which can occur very easily on these cars.

Rubber hedges were available to brighten up the trackside. Two stunningly rare cars are shown here in front of the hand-painted hedges and spectators. On the left is the production blue Type 59 Bugatti from the 1960s, which tended to overheat and melt so a lot of them were returned to the shop and discarded. The car appeared in six catalogues from the fourth to the ninth volumes and was only available by mail order for most of this time, with a few being assembled in batches once enough orders were received. On the right is the pre-production Type 59 Bugatti made around 1980 to test the moulds with the intention to reissue the car. However, this was never done, so this is actually a 'pre-non-production' car and there are only two or three of these in the world.

Rubber hay bales and a patch of grass on which to stand your Scalextric spectators and marshals beside the track – these were sold as Track Safety Barriers.

Rubber bushes and Goodwood wall: the Goodwood chicane first appeared in the version shown with a rubber wall secured to the track by plastic half-tyres and two rubber bushes. It was soon replaced by a version with all-plastic accessories, which didn't look anywhere near so nice. The cars shown are both Alfa Romeos and both are rare – the yellow one is the French version and the red one is a limited edition of the later 'Racing Classics' version with a blade guide.

Bridge Embankment – the rarest Scalextric accessory, and one of the rarest Scalextric items. These tapered hedges were expensive to buy, and so hardly anyone bought them (16*s* 5*d* in 1963 – equivalent to around £30 today). That together with the inherent fragility of all the rubber accessories means that there are hardly any left, especially in their boxes. You will pay many hundreds of pounds for a pair of these – if you can find them! (Picture courtesy Jenny Burrell)

Early English Boxes

The boxes in which the first plastic cars were sold were of the two-piece design, with a lift off lid. These are very strong and many thousands still remain in excellent condition. The second generation flip-top box does not survive so well but there are still a huge number out there in reasonable condition. Some cars never had boxes – the most notable being the vintage Type 59 Bugatti, which it is believed was sent out in a Juniors box.

The two-piece box shown here was used for the plastic cars at the start of Tri-ang's reign. Made of very thick card, they have withstood the rigours of the years very well and many are still in good condition. Reproduction ones abound, but are easy to spot as they are much too shiny and clean and don't have any scuffs, nor the tell-tale sixties Sellotape marks at each end, as shown in the photograph. The 1960s vintage English 'blower' Bentley is pictured alongside its original box.

Later Tri-ang introduced the flip-top cardboard box, which is much more flimsy and quite often the lid becomes detached. But if you can find one still in its original packing box, like this, then the box inside should be better preserved. The original 1964 price is pencilled on the label: 29/6 (29*s* 6*d*).

Early Sets

The first sets with plastic cars still had the old rubber track, but this changed to Plexytrack after it became available in 1963.

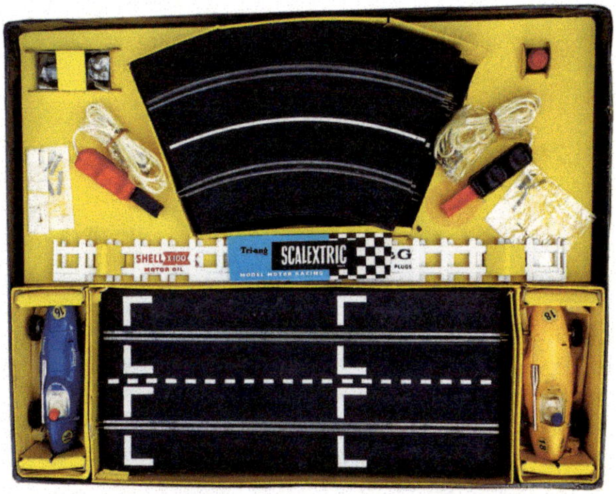

An almost perfect GP2 set from 1961 or 1962. The Vanwalls have the later small head drivers and therefore also have round guides. The track is rubber. The Shell oil bottle is unopened at the top right and top left is the bag of metal track clips that hold the track together to stop the electrical connections coming apart.

A CM3 set with two D-type Jaguars and a figure-of-eight circuit made up of the rubber track. The original tissue paper protecting the cars is still in their containers at the top left and right. The Shell oil bottle to the bottom left has been opened so you can see the cork.

The cardboard flyover supports from the CM3 set are the early unprinted version shown on the left. The first printed ones are shown on the right. These were soon superseded by the brightly coloured ones shown in the Juniors set at the beginning of the book.

The box artwork on the well-used lid of a V3 set.

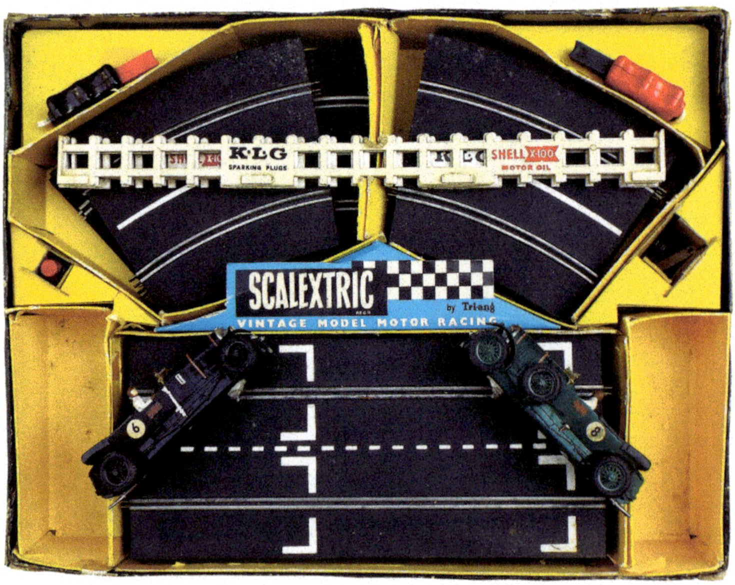

The V3 set with its original black and green blower Bentley cars. These cars still have their numbers and Union Jack stickers in place, and their original fish-tail exhaust pipes. Cars in sets like this should look old, and the chrome should be faded, but still being in original condition they look and feel right.

GK1 go-kart set. The box lid artwork is very good, and the two karts are the early ones with grey guides and wheels, and are fitted with plastic underpans that cover the motor. These were quickly discarded as the karts overheated and they worked much better without them.

If you are looking to purchase a Scalextric go-kart, make sure it has all the components still attached to its engines – carburettors, spark plugs and exhausts – like this one. This is the later version without the underpan.

MC1 set with two Typhoon motorcycle combinations and rubber hump back bridge. Because this was the only set which included the rubber hump back bridge, it became known as the 'Typhoon Bridge'. Each one was supplied with the carved piece of wood shown between the two machines. This fitted exactly into the ribs of the hump section beneath the track, thereby supporting it and preventing it from getting flattened by an inadvertent footstep.

Original Spares

The fun of hunting around on the spares rack was one of the joys of the weekly visit to the toy shop. Many original spares can still be found, some unopened, but modern copies (reproduction spares) are good imitations and you need to be careful if you are seeking the real thing.

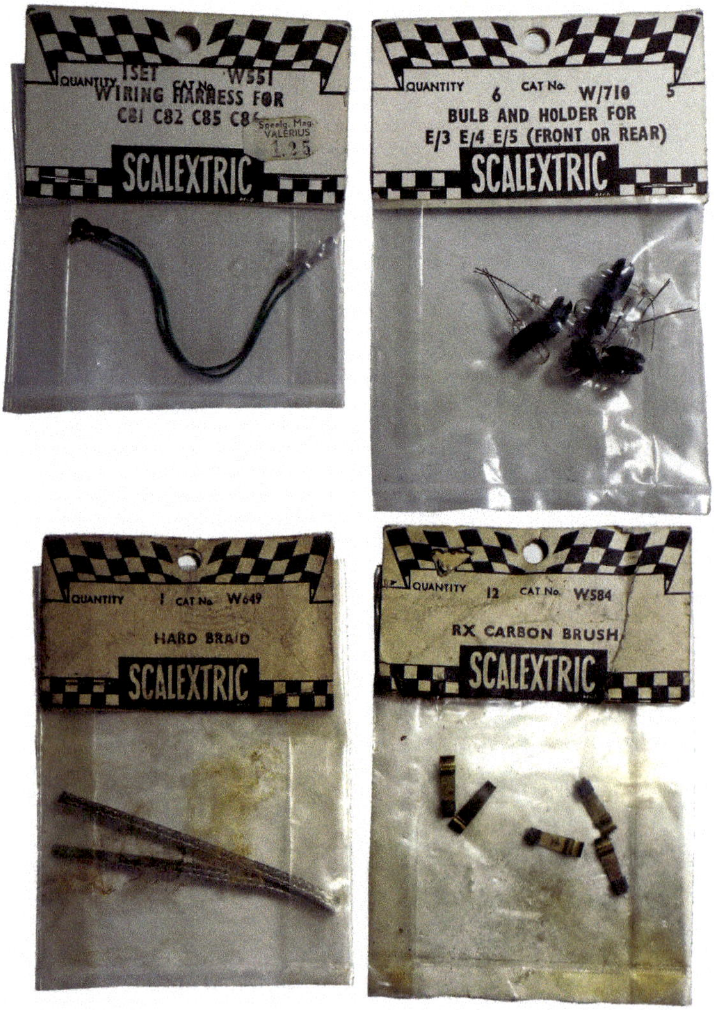

English Scalextric spares in their original packets. The wiring harness is for one of four of the later Junior type cars – Cooper, Lotus, BRM and Porsche. The bulbs and their holders top right are for the Ferrari 250 and Aston Martin DB4 (normal and Marshal versions). The spares shown at the bottom are the most often needed – braids for the pick-ups and brushes for the RX motors.

People

Lots of sets of 1/32 scale spectators and circuit officials and drivers and race-day vendors were produced, and feature in many of the photographs in this book. The Super124 series of cars and track also had its own people in 1/24 scale and these take a lot of seeking out.

The set of 1/32 scale drivers and mechanics in their unopened box.

The set of 1/24 scale drivers in their box. This set is very rare and sells for many hundreds of pounds. (Picture courtesy Jenny Burrell)

Sounds

From early on the factory released various systems for creating authentic racing engine sounds, and two of them are pictured here. Before any of these, the first soundtrack was released on a 45 rpm vinyl single called *Roar!* This had one side for playing racing car noises and the other for TT motorcycles.

Twin Auto-Screams was designed to give realistic engine sounds by pressing an extra switch mounted on the early (thumb-type) hand controller.

The Sound Track system was wired to the hand controller cables and so adjusted the sounds according to power – a much better system than the Auto-Screams.

The Mini Becomes Rear-Wheel-Drive

As stated earlier, the attempt at front-wheel-drive on the Scalextric Mini was a bit of a flop, so a rear-wheel-drive version was brought out with the standard size RX motor and layout. This was much more successful and was produced in dozens of different versions over the years, from Cooper to Clubman to Metro, many of which are shown in this book.

Two Monte Carlo Mini Coopers in their element. These are the rear-wheel-drive version of the Mini, which replaced the front-wheel-drive one described earlier.

Modern Copies of Old Classics

On many occasions the factory produced versions of old models that had been deleted from the catalogue, sometimes using the same moulds, but maybe with a modern guide (as in the illustration below), and sometimes with new tooling, so the result is more accurate.

Vintage cars, two blue, old and new. The nearer one is the English vintage Alfa Romeo (contrast this with the French yellow one shown earlier). The Bentley behind is a modern version in the 'Racing Classics' series with a blade guide brought out at the same time as the red Alfa Romeo also shown earlier with the yellow Alfa.

Scalextric Juniors – So Many to Choose From

Juniors were released as a budget version of the Scalextric car with a smaller motor and simple but not very detailed body. They were all modelled on single-seat racing cars and sold in their thousands – mainly, I suspect, because when asked for a Scalextric set for Christmas, most parents went for the ones that were two thirds of the price! That was certainly how I came by my own FJ31 set. The variation of colours and body types among Juniors is vast, and there are people who are experts on the subject. The following pictures give a flavour of what is available.

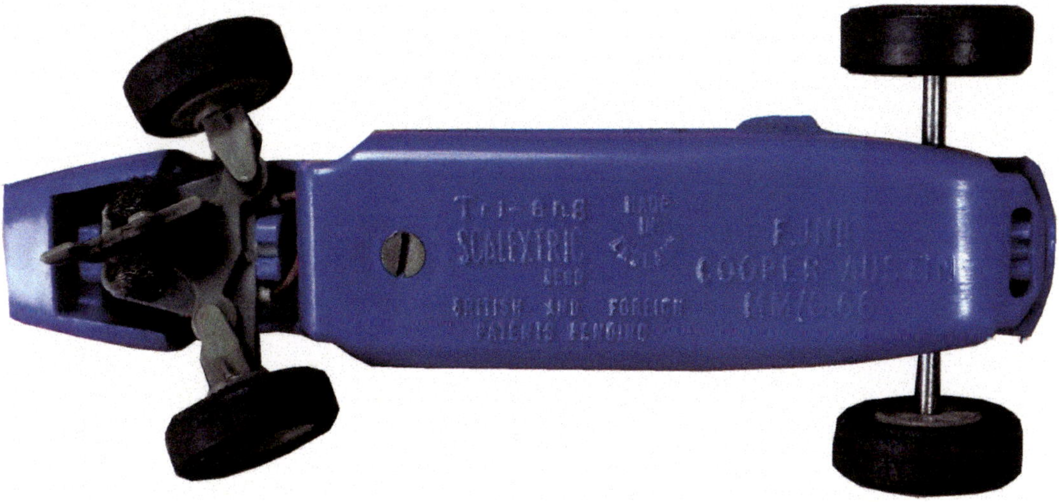

The first Juniors had grey guide and steering and a screw holding the front of the underpan. This type of Junior is now commonly known as 'screw-base'.

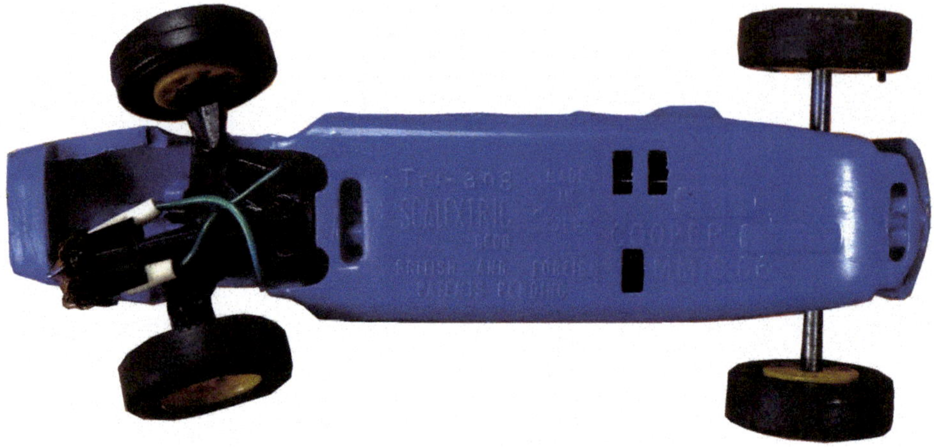

The later Junior base, which clips on at the front and rear. The later black guide and steering are also visible.

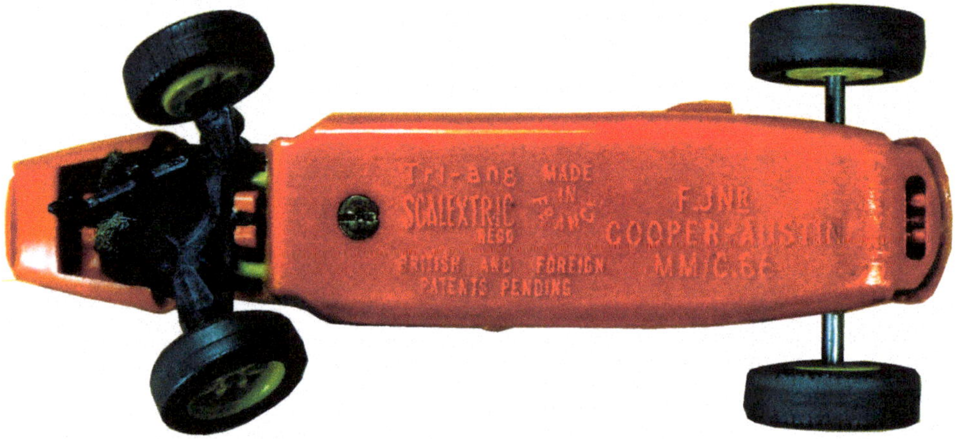

A French screw-base Junior with black guide and steering.

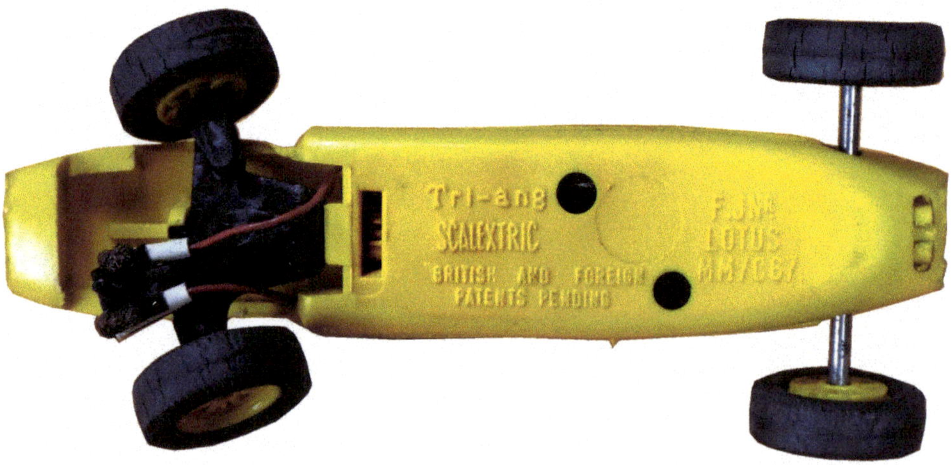

Another French Junior, this one with clip-on base and two cooling holes for the motor.

An interesting assortment of Juniors. The red car front left is a French Lotus with a racing stripe on its nose. Behind it is another French Lotus, this time the later one, but in the rare orange colour. The green car is a Porsche Junior and this is in the rare green colour for this model. The two yellow cars are the original old-shape Cooper (top left) and Lotus (top right), but in an unusual colour produced only in France. Although it is difficult to tell in the picture, these cars are made from translucent plastic so if you hold them up to the light they glow. They are considerably rarer than other Juniors and therefore more expensive.

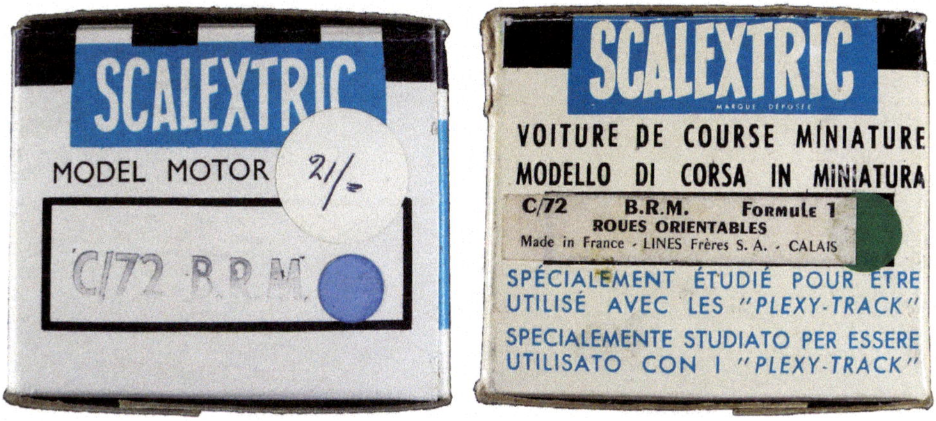

Two Juniors boxes for the C/72 BRM – one English and one French. The English car cost 21*s* as you can see. The French car has some encouragement on the box for intending purchasers, telling them that these cars are designed specially to work on the newly introduced flexible plastic track 'PLEXY-TRACK'. It also states that the car has 'ROUES ORIENTABLES' (steerable wheels).

Cars Made Overseas

Early French Cars: The Calais Connection

From the very beginning of Tri-ang Minimodels plastic car production in Havant, a French facility was opened in Calais. This produced the same cars using, at the start, the same moulds. It then went on to design and make French-only cars, but many were sold in Britain and Spain and other parts of the world. Because of the confusion of moulds, it is difficult to tell which early cars are definitely from the Calais factory and which are English. If the cars are of a colour only produced by the French for that model of car, then this makes the task simpler. Some of the cars are stamped 'MADE IN FRANCE', or 'FABRIQUE EN FRANCE', thus leaving no doubt about their origin. However, some with a blank country of manufacture mark, and even some with 'MADE IN ENGLAND' on them, are definitely French. The accompanying pictures show and describe what to look out for.

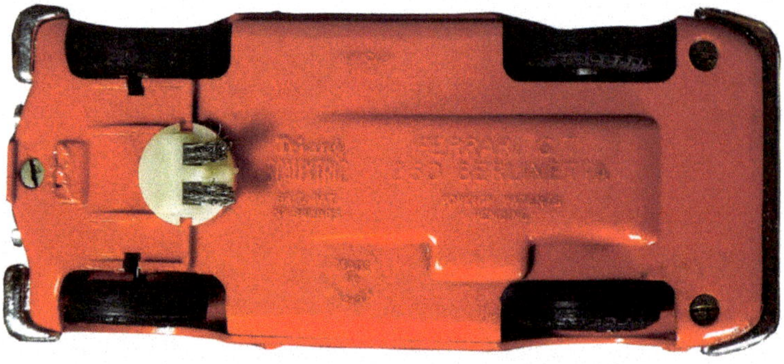

Here is a French Ferrari 250 – it is easy to tell as it says 'MADE IN FRANCE' on the base. Note the opaque white guide, which was fitted to many of the French cars.

Here is a French Vanwall – this one says 'FABRIQUE EN FRANCE', which gives complete certainty as to its country of origin.

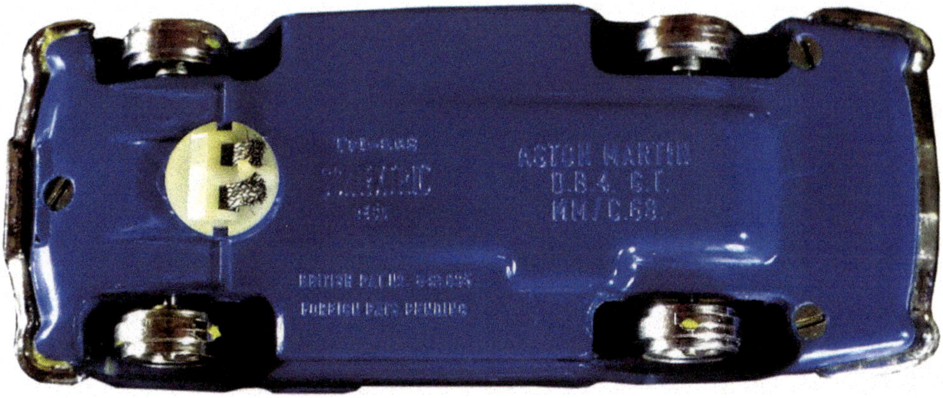

This Aston Martin DB4 has the roundel where it usually says 'MADE IN …' blanked out. Cars with a blank like this could have been made in France, or they could have been made in England for sale in France or Germany or Australia. However, there are other clues which we can use. In this example, the colour means that this is a French car – blue DB4s were only made in Calais. This car also has the whiter opaque round guide which is a French characteristic.

This is a French Aston Martin DB4. It says 'MADE IN ENGLAND' on the base, but it is definitely French because only Calais made the DB4 in yellow. This is because when the Calais factory was set up, they initially used moulds brought over from England and simply produced cars using the English moulds.

These are black and green blower Bentleys and they are French. The French Bentleys have tan colour tonneau covers and red wheels. The English tonneau covers are grey, and the wheels are the same colour as the car. The green of the French Bentley is much brighter than the English green. The French cars are altogether much more *jolie* than the English ones.

The English and French front-engined Lotus. The red car is the later French version with contrasting colour for the exhaust and mirrors and rear springs.

The cars from the French set 60 (with lights). These colours were both only made in France – a green Ferrari 250 and blue Aston Martin DB4.

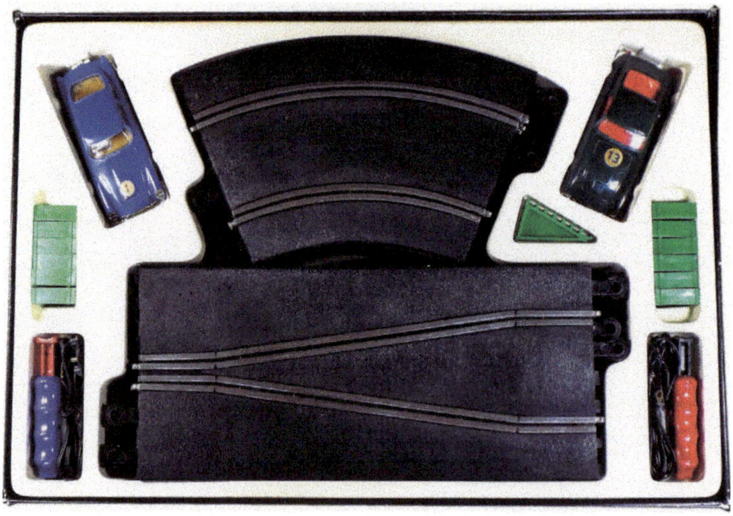

The set 60 in its box. French set boxes differ from the English ones: they have a plastic tray instead of cardboard inserts and the box lids are made of thicker card, which makes them much more resilient. All the items in the box are stamped 'MADE IN FRANCE', including the track and hand controllers.

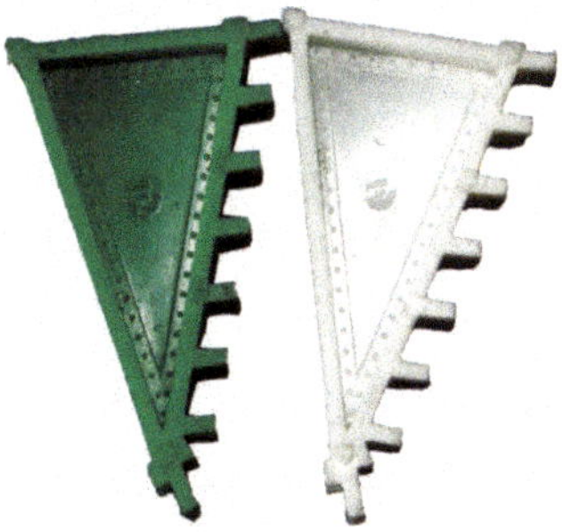

Above left: The banking wedges in French sets are also stamped with their country of origin. French banking wedges are either in a brighter green than the English ones, or in white, as shown in the picture.

Above right: The Renault 12 was one of the very few Scalextric cars to be fitted with weights to hold it down on the track (the Porsche Spyder as described earlier is one, the Renault Alpine and Matra-Jet are others). The Renault weights are in the shape of cylindrical metal rods which clip into the plastic bodywork as shown.

The Renault 12 hits trouble in the snow, along with the Mini Clubman. A friendly neighbour in the Datsun 4x4 Hawaiian Cruiser has come to help out.

Two Alpine Renaults. The blue one is the earliest French-produced car using their own moulds and was never made in England. For this reason, it actually has the distinction of being number C/1 in the Scalextric model range. The French Matra-Jet, which was produced at the same time, is C/2. The first English cars started at C/54 so there must have been fifty-three gaps to fill and the Renault Alpine just happened to bag number. 1. The later Alpine is shown in red on the right. Another Renault Alpine was also modelled for Scalextric, but this time in Spain.

French Boxes

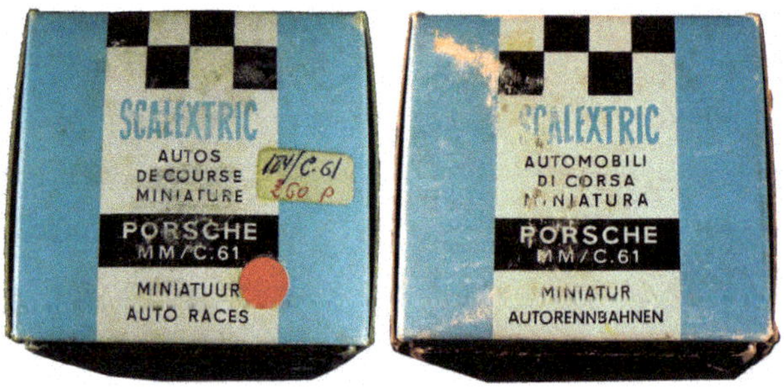

The early French box was a copy of the English two-piece one but with writing in four different languages: French and Dutch on one end, and Italian and German on the other.

This distinctive blue and red box proudly displayed that it contained a car made in France; this time the French black Bentley.

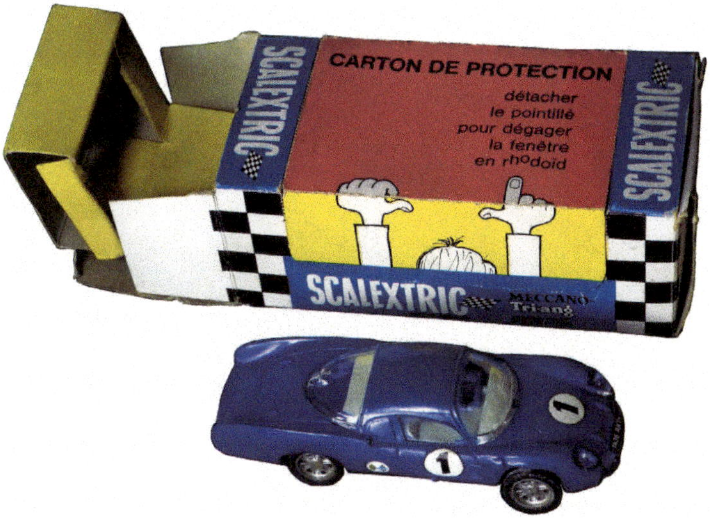

Later French boxes had perforations and a removable piece of card, which protected the cellophane window beneath. This is the box for the C/1 Alpine Renault.

French Racing Numbers

The font used on the roundels carrying the racing numbers of French cars often had a narrower font than those from England and are quite distinctive, as shown in the accompanying picture. However, the numbers used by the Calais factory at the very beginning were the English ones.

The French Aston Martin DB4 in yellow. This one has a slight brown mark over the wheel arch on the far side – very common with these cars. This makes it worth half that of an unblemished car, but it will still cost several hundred pounds. Note the French style of numbers on the roundels.

French Spares

French round guides were pure white and opaque on first manufacture, as shown by the pristine ones on the left. English round guides were paler and translucent. After years of storage the French ones go slightly yellower, as shown on the right, but are still easy to distinguish as they remain opaque and quite different when you see the two side-by-side.

Power Sledges – The Arrival of Speed

Power sledges are an important part of Scalextric history, because they were the first cars that went so fast you almost couldn't see them – especially when the body was removed and you just drove the skeleton around the track. They were the fastest things around until the arrival of Magnatraction in 1988 on the Williams and Lotus cars of Mansell and Senna. But actually, power sledges are more fun to drive because the tail hangs out on the corners. The later cars held down by magnets stick better when they are in line, but as soon as you do lose the tail they are off because the magnet is no longer over the steel conductor rails of the track and therefore all downforce is instantly lost. Many slot car racers remove the magnets from the cars to experience proper racing, or they just use power sledges instead! Modern super grippy tyres are now available for power sledges, which make them even faster than they were in their heyday.

At this time, the French factory was making almost everything that the English one did, and power sledges were no exception. Telling the English and French versions apart is not too difficult as they have differences that are easily spotted – the accompanying pictures show what to look for.

The English power sledge has a slot head screw and silver sided motor. The French power sledge has a crosshead screw and black sided motor, the armature windings of which are more orange coloured.

The English power sledge has a hole in the centre of the wheels and the driver's goggles are painted. The French power sledge has a no hole in the wheels and driver's goggles are unpainted.

The French Lotus Indianapolis power sledge with unpainted driver's goggles.

A white Lotus Indianapolis and a blue Ferrari – two of the colours produced by the French factory.

The French Matra with its box. Note the semi-circular loop at the back of the car – this is often missing from the Matra as it snaps off very easily.

A very rare green power sledge Matra.

The Spanish and Mexican Cars

Scalextric opened a Tri-ang-owned factory in Calais around 1960, but getting a facility in Spain was more difficult because of the political situation and the fact that General Franco was in power. Initially, the Spanish toy manufacturer Exin simply imported French and English Scalextric cars and sold them in Spain. They later designed and built their own models of car and sold them as Scalextric under licence from Tri-ang.

These are easier to identify than the French cars, as all Spanish cars say 'MADE IN SPAIN' on the base. Exin also had a factory in Mexico and the Mexican-made cars have 'HECHO EN MEXICO' on the base.

Many Spanish cars were of models and makes only produced by Exin, so some appeared in the British catalogue and were imported to the UK, such as the Seat 600 and Mercedes 250SL. Others, such as the archetypally British E-type Jaguar, were imported as body parts and assembled in Britain, stating as such on the box ends.

Many Spanish cars are available for the collector, and they are beautifully made and accurately modelled, especially detailed ones such as the P34 six-wheel Tyrrell Formula One car. They quite often still have their original Spanish boxes, which are very robust and are usually in superb condition.

The Mexican cars appear either to have had harder lives, or the plastic used was not as good quality as that used for their Spanish sisters, seeing as they tend to warp and have bits missing. Talking of the plastic, the Spanish cars smell different from the English and French ones – you will notice when you first get one. The Mexican cars are slightly more pungent again.

The very first Scalextric car produced by the Exin factory in Barcelona was the tiny Seat 600, which in real life was the Spanish version of the Italian Fiat 500 Cinquecento. The picture shows the common red-coloured car and the very rare grey version. Other colours are white, which is common, and pale green, which is rare (*see page 93*).

The Spanish made a very nice model of the Renault Alpine, an open-top sports racing car.

This picture shows two versions of the 1970s Formula One Tyrrell 001 as raced by Jackie Stewart in 1970 before it received a rounded nose cone and became the 003, which he drove to the world driver's title in 1973. One is the contemporary Spanish Exin model and the other is a modern Scalextric issue of the same car. The Spanish cars were so well modelled in the 1970s that it is hard to tell which is which. The red car is the Spanish one.

The fabulous Ford Mustang and Chevrolet Corvette dragsters in a night-time burn-out.

The STS (SuperTrack System) with four-wheel-drive Jeeps. These sets have a rough terrain track with built-in tyre tracks for extra grip and the cars, with worm drive to all four wheels, can climb very steep hills. The smell of these sets when you open the box is quite extraordinary, being very strong and overpowering – presumably because of the type of plastic that was used.

The *Manual de Instrucciones* (Instruction Manual) gives an example of a layout that can be created using the STS track – and it looks very impressive!

Spanish Boxes

The standard blue and green box used by Exin for its Scalextric cars. The cardboard is laminated and lasts very well. This one contains a blue six-wheel Tyrrell P-34 and is complete with instruction leaflet.

The later box used by Exin for models sold in countries outside Spain. This one has the same P-34 Tyrrell in green – the cellophane has been removed so the car can be seen more clearly.

Spanish Spares

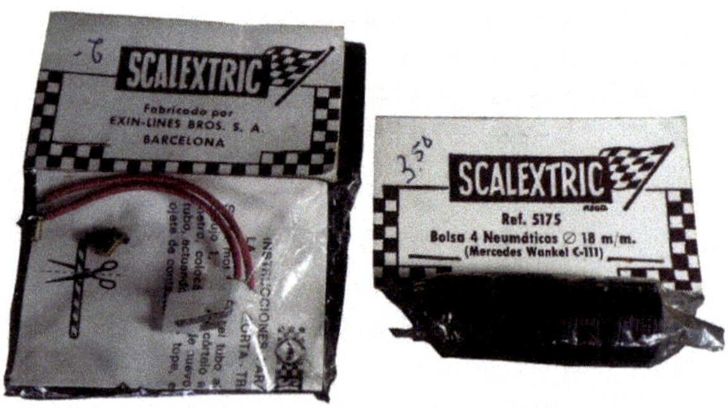

A standard Spanish blade guide and a set of new tyres for the Mercedes Wankel.

Mexican Cars and Sets

It is much more difficult to find Mexican cars than Spanish ones, and consequently good original ones are rare. There is a flourishing business in refurbishing Mexican cars, but these usually have reproduction parts and decals/stickers. Many strange colours of various models were produced by ExinMex and these sell for high prices.

This picture enables us to compare three different versions of the same car – the 1960s Cooper Climax. The blue car is the original early '60s Scalextric Junior car produced in vast quantities in both England and France. Behind it is the Mexican version, made in the early '70s. Car No. 1 is the modern, highly detailed Scalextric Cooper, which was made in the 2010s.

Fabulous box artwork for the Mexican GP.65 set with two Corvette dragsters.

The inside of the GP.65 set. It is most unusual to find a Mexican set in this complete and unused condition. The transformer is included in the set and looks highly dangerous! The finish banner has wooden posts to support it and is made of a cloth-reinforced vinyl.

These two ExinMex Corvette dragsters are just about perfect, with just some tiny flakes coming off the flame decals at the front.

Hong Kong, Australia and the USSR

Cars made in Hong Kong were sold in large numbers in all parts of the world, including the UK, but only in a limited range of models. Common Hong Kong cars are the two versions of the Offenhauser Indianapolis car – front-engined and rear-engined – as well as the Lamborghini Miura pictured earlier and the AC Cobra pictured here, along with the Ford GT40.

Australia produced its own sets and cars made under licence by Moldex, but it also had special versions of cars that were made in Britain and sold in Australia.

There were even two cars manufactured in the USSR – the Ford Mirage and Lamborghini Miura. These were the cars in the 'Novo' slot racing sets sold in Russia at that time, but they were also sold individually and many can be found in the UK and elsewhere. They are not usually expensive, unless they are in a rare colour.

Right: The AC Cobra was made in Hong Kong and sold all around the world. The 1960s price was 21*s*.

Below: This Palmer Tube Mills Mk 3 Ford Escort was made in England for export to Australia. The bumpers fitted to the English version are black and the Australian ones are green.

Before black became the standard colour for banking wedges in Britain, Australian Scalextric manufacturer Moldex was already making them in the 1960s.

Two 1970s cars were made in the USSR (now Russia). This is the Lamborghini Miura.

Television and Movie Cars

James Bond

It took several years before Scalextric signed its first licensing deal with a television or film company to produce a themed set. In 1967 *James Bond* appeared, charging around a figure-of-eight crossover layout, pursued by gangsters in a Black Mercedes 190. This set is now rare and highly desirable, especially if it hasn't been messed about with – almost the whole thing is available as reproduction items: box lid, inner card trays, figures, sun roof, plastic rock etc.There are two forms of the Aston Martin DB4 car, as described in the accompanying photograph. Pictured below is another *James Bond* DB4, which isn't a factory item but is possibly unique.

Why are these sets so rare? The problem was the track configuration and the function of the cars meant that they were designed to hit each other – and presumably did so quite often, and at high speed. This meant that after being played with on Christmas Day, the cars were smashed to pieces, so the frustrated parents took the whole thing back to the shop. The ones that did survive usually had lots of bits broken off, which is why a good intact one is a very nice find for a *James Bond*-craving Scalextric fanatic. It is now almost certainly the most expensive set, although prices have been coming down.

The cars from the 007 *James Bond* set are a white Aston Martin DB4 with machine guns poking from the holes where the spotlights would be on the standard car, a bulletproof shield which pops up at the back, and of course the sunroof and working ejector seat. The black Mercedes 190 'baddie' car has a spring underneath, which rolls the car over when it is hit from behind.

The 007 set is probably the most desirable set for the collector. There are three loose figures in the set and a plastic 'rock', which is placed in a hole in the 007 track, which is hidden beneath the card cover at the bottom left. The arrows on the track show that the 007 Aston Martin must be placed on that side and run in the direction indicated so that the ejector seat mechanism comes in contact with the plastic rock as the car drives past. The three figures rock, and sunroof are often missing and there are lots of reproduction ones around. Genuine original figures will be worn with some paint missing, and most of the paint on the rock will be rubbed away by the car hitting it. Genuine instructions will be aged, as shown.

This picture is for comparison of the earlier and later 007 Aston Martin cars. The early one on the left is assembled using slot head brass machine screws, which screw into brass inserts in the plastic body. The later car uses crosshead self-tapping screws, which locate directly into the plastic. This version is much more common as it was cheaper to make.

What have we here? James Bond goes into the red? This is not a re-sprayed 007 car but a sunroof version of a red DB4 that has been remodelled into the 007 car with working bulletproof shield and an ejector seat, courtesy Richard Johnson.

Spiderman

Spiderman sets did not arrive until 1984, but when they did they gave us a splash of colour in red and yellow-decorated Triumph TR7 cars, and a pure white track on which to run them.

The *Spiderman* set has its own white track and two Triumph TR7 cars. The white track is more brittle than the standard black and the locating lugs often snap off – take care when assembling, and also especially when taking apart. The car was also sold as a 'lights down' version, with only half of Spiderman pictured on the bonnet.

M.A.S.K.

M.A.S.K was a Japanese animation in which the good guys from Mobile Armoured Strike Kommand fought the Vicious Evil Network of Mayhem (V.E.N.O.M.).

The M.A.S.K. Thunderhawk (red car) and V.E.N.O.M. Manta (purple car), which are the Pontiac Firebirds in the M.A.S.K. Patrol set.

Knight Rider

Michael Knight is a crime fighter whose car, K.I.T.T (Knight Industries Two Thousand), has artificial intelligence and does a lot of the thinking and crime-fighting for him. K.I.T.T has a special coating and is virtually indestructible – the Scalextric version is much the same, having no protuberances that can snap off and black livery all over. It's very hard to find a broken one!

K.I.T.T (Pontiac Firebird TransAm) and Datsun 260Z from the *Knight Rider* sets.

Batman

The caped crusader arrived in his Batmobile on a Scalextric track in 1990, pitted against his foremost enemy, The Joker, who drove a pink Porsche Carrera.

This is a line-up of the standard Batman and Joker cars from the first sets, plus two very rare and unusual Batmobiles – one in clear plastic and the other green.

Teenage Mutant Ninja Turtles

A year after *Batman*, the pizza-eating, drain-dwelling heroes in a half-shell arrived. In two of the sets they were on motorised skateboards, and in the other set (pictured) they get bigger transport to carry out their super deeds.

Green TURTLES track with the Datsun 4x4 and hot-rodded van from the Turtles to the Rescue set. The van does not have its red 'drain cover lifting' accessories fitted as these are still in the box on their sprue.

Power Rangers

For lovers of karate kids in cat suits on motorbikes, what could be better? *Power Rangers* motorcycle combinations in their multi-coloured finery really are great things to collect, and not too expensive. They drive fast and well too.

The multi-coloured *Power Rangers* motorcycles with Tommy and Trini (green), Billy and Kimberly (blue), Zack and Kimberly (black) and Jason and Trini (red) – Trini being shown with a different crash helmet in the red motorcycle as the original probably fell off.

Starsky and Hutch and *Transformers*

These two television series probably never met in artificial life, but on the Scalextric track anything goes. The *Starsky and Hutch* set originally had a black Corvette for the villains, but this was replaced by a white one later in the run. *Transformers* was a set only in Micro-Scalextric, but Bumblebee was produced, as shown here, in 1/32 scale.

Ford Camaro Bumblebee hanging out on the bridge, watching Starsky and Hutch in the Ford Gran Torino, overtaking the later white Corvette. The one in the first sets was black.

Disney *Cars*

Lightning McQueen and Francesco Bernoulli from the Disney Cars 2 World Grand Prix set. The set was branded 'Start' as the track was a budget range produced for a few years alongside the Sport track system. Start track did not prove that popular, but with adapters it can be used with the current Sport track. The two cars are also available in Disney-branded boxes – these are quite hard to find now in unused condition because they were played with so much by their young drivers.

Dukes of Hazzard

The Dodge Charger *General Lee* driven by Bo and Luke, the Dukes of Hazzard in the television series of the same name.

Two Dead Ends that Helped Put Tri-ang out of Business

Super 124

Super124 cars are 1/24 scale and as a result were expensive to make. The track they were supplied with has three lanes and the rails are made of stainless steel so they can be used outdoors. Tri-ang invested heavily – too heavily – in making these cars and sets, in the belief that slot car clubs all over the country would be set up using Super124, but it never happened. We are left with a legacy of some beautiful cars in large scale, however, and the two single-seater racing cars are especially prized. The sports cars in this scale are most prone to warping and often if you look along the sides of these cars the bowing is quite obvious.

The Super 124 cars were not made in large quantities and are of very high quality, although they are prone to warping. Here we have the cheapest Super 124 you can buy – the Alfa Romeo in blue – and one of the most expensive – the beautiful V8 Ferrari 158 Grand Prix car in which John Surtees won the Formula One driver's championship in 1964.

You Steer

You Steer – well, what can we say about it? You have a perfectly good product that tens of thousands of people are buying every year and you think 'this would be even better if we put bollards in the middle of the road and cardboard tunnels and you have to steer round them'. And maybe, if the engineers had come up with a way of steering the cars that wasn't simply dreadful, then you may have been right. But the solution was anything but. You take a standard car and put a strange rotating screw at the back driven by the motor. On this screw is a long arm that projects to the front and carries the guide and braids. When you want to 'steer' the car, you turn a wheel on the hand controller, which reverses the polarity of the current to the car. The motor has to stop spinning at 10,000 rpm or whatever, then reverse itself to spin in the opposite direction, thus changing the direction of the screw and moving the guide, but not the direction of the car. So basically, steering made you stop, then go again. Even a child wouldn't put up with that. And they didn't.

The You Steer conversion set, perfect with flagpole and accessories (not illustrated), bought for less than £20. Give it a go and see how bad it really is!

Police and Marshal Cars

Police cars have always been popular with collectors and there are plenty to choose from, including some rare pre-production and Code 3 models.

Marshal cars were originally based on the Aston Martin DB4 from the 1960s and are the front and rear-lighted version with the addition of a roof light. The English made only black ones, while the French made them in black, red and green. Later Marshal cars were a Rover SD1 and a Vectra.

The dastardly Joker is finally run to ground – and it takes eight police cars to do so. Attending the crash scene is a selection of police cars that have been released over the years. Most have working flashing lights and many have a working siren as well. The two versions of the black and white Audi R8 on the left of the picture may look the same on first inspection, but HH01 is from the Law Enforcer set and HH18 is the solo release. No. 641 is the silver Subaru that was perhaps caught up in the Joker chase as it has lost its nearside mirror. The pale blue and white Mini with the Welsh police word Heddlu tampoed on the bonnet can also be found as a Code 3 model as a limited run of 100 for a swapmeet. Alongside the Mini is the blue Lamborghini Gallardo. Behind it is a prototype of the Alfa Romeo police car that was eventually released in a green livery. Behind the Mini is a white Ford Sierra. At the rear is the Range Rover, which is available in conventional and drift (360 degree guide) versions, though the bodyshell is decorated exactly the same. Because they were often sold in sets, certain police models can be found more easily than others and there is a wide spread of prices between different models of the same car. Perhaps the most limited (and expensive) factory release to seek out is the C2120 Jersey CrimeStoppers Vectra, which was produced in a small run of just 500 cars.

The 1960s Scalextric Aston Martin DB4 Marshal car in black, with its original flags, attends the scene of an accident in which Jo Siffert in his Yardley BRM is caught on a telegraph pole. The yellow Marshal car in the foreground is customised from a C/7 Mini Cooper, courtesy of Richard Johnson.

Hanging on the bushes, which are just saving him from plummeting into the canyon below, is Clay Regazzoni in his Ferrari. He is attended by a black Marshal car – but it is not an Aston Martin, instead being a customised Ferrari 250 – and another Marshal driving a Fiat 850. Both are courtesy of Richard Johnson.

Attending the scene of the crashed and now roofless Mini is an '80s yellow Rover SD1 Marshal's car and a black F1 Track Marshal Vectra car. The Track Marshal car was available initially through the Hornby-run collectors' club alongside white Paramedic and red Fire Marshal versions of the Vectra. While the black Track Marshal is still relatively easy to find today, the Rover is much scarcer, especially complete with its original flags.

Motorcycles

The early motorcycle combinations are probably the most difficult thing to drive that ever graced a slot car track. The tyres are about 2 mm wide, and the distance between them and the guide pin is about 2 inches (50 mm). They are belt-driven from a pulley on the end of a sidewinder motor, but are great fun. They were available in either left- or right-hand-drive versions. Later motorcycle combinations had a motor mounted lengthways along the chassis with a crown gear on the back axle and wide slick tyres, so they handle very well. In addition to the ones shown in the picture here, there are also the *Power Rangers* versions pictured earlier (*see page 70*). The solo motorcycles have a plastic skid beneath them to keep them upright. Considering that the back wheel is always on top of the metal rails and slot of the track, they are stunningly fast and do not suffer from the expected wheel-spin. Set up a long straight track, as long as possible, and they will be doing a ridiculous speed by the end of it, but will never take the first bend without falling off unless throttled back halfway down the straightaway. They are great models and very detailed.

This picture shows some of the range of motorcycles produced. The green Typhoon is the later (and rarer) version with a front wheel – all the earlier Typhoons have a skid instead. The yellow Hurricane is the left-hand-drive version of the Typhoon and this is the rarest colour. All Hurricanes have a front wheel. The red sidecar outfit is the 1980 release, which has wide slick tyres and the motor in line with the body. Two of these were included in the 500TT set. The solo motorcycle is one of around twenty-four different variations produced in the 2000s – this one is a MotoGP Ducati ridden by Neil Hodgson. They are very accurately modelled and incredibly fast in a straight line, but the cornering is tricky to say the least. They were soon dropped from the range and are very nice items to collect, and are not yet too expensive.

Badges, Medals, Mugs and Prizes

There have been many items produced by Scalextric over the years for sale and used as promotional items for events and competitions. This has included pens, badges, keyrings, balloons, T-shirts, special cars and medals. There are official Scalextric items of merchandise and giveaway items, plus many, many more produced by individual clubs and for promoting festivals. Here is a selection.

Right: The 1960s Scalextric driver's brooch was produced in large numbers. This is a complete card of twelve of them, as would have been seen hanging on the spares rack in the 1960s toyshop. In 1964 they sold for 4*d* each. This is a very rare item in this condition and complete – even the hole they hung by has not been punched out.

Below: The medal shown was given as a junior prize in the 1964 German Scalextric championship.

Above: Assorted Scalextric badges and merchandise. Top row: Scalextric pen; employee service badge which reads 'ROVEX SCALE MODELS' and the number 5, so probably for five years' service; and Scalextric keyring. Middle row: Spanish competition badge; brass hand throttle keyring; and Scalextric 50th anniversary badge (Spanish). Bottom row: Scalextric marketing badge; Scalextric Start badge which reads '…let the race begin!'; two NSCC badges; and Driver's cloth badge.

Left: Celebrate after the race with a mug of Scalextric coffee. Many designs of mug were made for various events and collectors' clubs. Only some mugs were made or officially licensed by Scalextric – there are many others for sale on the internet.

Right: The presentation trophy set has three cups for winner, runner-up and third place, plus a laurel wreath for the victor. Here it is unopened on its card at a cost of 4*s* 6*d*.

Below: Sometimes the factory made special editions of cars to give away as prizes at competitions. This is a gorgeous round guide vintage blower Bentley with gold body and silver wheels, with the underpan in perfect condition. They were all made in France and therefore do not have 'MADE IN ENGLAND' on the base – however, there are many fakes about. Imagine John Steed rocking up to the door of Elvedon Manor in one of these.

Club, Swapmeet, Slot-Car Festival, Range Presentation Cars and Livery Variations

This section shows a large selection of more modern cars that have been decorated either by the factory or as Code 3 for special events and range presentations.

The Aston Martin sports saloon was first produced as the DB4 in the 1960s. The modern version is a DB5 and is just as collectible. Here are examples of red DB5s that have been decorated for the Dutch SLN collectors' club (left) and the 2017 UK Slot Car Festival (centre). The standard release car is on the right. The Marshal version sold out in minutes at the UKSF and is now generally more expensive than the original '60s black Marshal car.

Like the Aston Martin DB5, the E-type Jaguar is another popular car for decorating. Here, examples from the UK Slot Car Festival and Dutch SLN club lead the regular released car through the bridge.

The No. 6 white E-type is one of fifty produced for the 2018 UK Slot Car Festival while the No. 4 car is one of 125 produced for the same event. The regular Scalextric release has the number 9 (C3890). The red E-type is the original Scalextric car made in the late '60s/early '70s. However, although an iconic British car, it was never manufactured in Britain – the Spanish Exin factory produced the moulds and when the car was sold in Britain the box stated that it contained foreign parts. As with all the Exin cars, it is a beautiful model, especially the genuine Spanish ones in their blue and green boxes.

In 1998 Scalextric started producing a limited run of cars for dealers at the start of each new year classified as 'Range Presentation' cars in individually numbered boxes. While initially attracting a lot of interest from collectors, examples can be bought now for a small premium over the price of the latest releases. The picture shows the 1998 Lamborghini Diablo in gold, which looks very attractive if you can get one where the gold paintwork has not crazed.

Orange cars have been produced in greater numbers over recent years with small differences between models. There are several Porsches available in orange, while the picture shows four of the many orange Lamborghini Gallardos produced in 'impact resistant' form.

The picture shows factory examples of the Audi R8 produced with slightly different printing for the NSCC/Hornby weekend in 2011 (front right) and the Scalextric Official Club Car (left) of the same year. Bringing up the rear is a Chaparral produced by the factory for the NSCC (National Scalextric Collectors' Club).

During 2012 Scalextric produced a number of sky blue McLaren MP4-12C liveries, with the UK Slot Car Festival (left), Range Presentation (middle) and the Dutch SLN club car (right) being shown in the picture. Alongside these are three liveries of the Mercedes SLR McLaren from 2010, showing the Range Presentation car No. 12, Dutch SLN car No. 1 and NSCC car No. 11.

The snow effect Ferrari P4 shown in red in the picture was produced by the factory in very limited numbers and was sent out to journalists as a promotional item – it is now very sought after by collectors. In 2010 the NSCC (National Scalextric Collectors' Club) commissioned a run of 750 Jaguars (shown in green) to celebrate their 30th anniversary. The cars came in the factory crystal-case box but were repackaged into a presentation box with card by the NSCC. A small number of the 30th Anniversary NSCC Jaguars were then taken by the NSCC club, decorated with a snow effect, and were then sold at a small premium to club members to help with sales of that particular model. These Jaguars still have the original limited edition card in the NSCC-packaged box indicating a run of 750 cars, but it is believed that only around fifty snowy versions were actually produced.

This MG Metro 6R4 is one of a run of 100 decorated in snow-effect commissioned by the organisers of the Swindon swapmeet event in 2016. The livery depicts the car leaving 'Parc Fermé' following the Lombard RAC rally in 1986.

There have been many models that have been produced by Hornby in small limited runs for the NSCC (National Scalextric Collectors' Club), SLN (Dutch Collectors' Club) and ASRCC (Australian Scalextric Racing and Collecting Club), as well as some companies and organisations like the UKSF (UK Slot Car Festival), over the past couple of decades. However, because Scalextric has moved away from small production runs during the twenty-first century, and with the advances in technology for tampo printing and decal production, there have been increasing numbers of cars produced by the aforementioned organisations and clubs as Code 3 models for specific events, designed to appeal to collectors and to fill the gap that the manufacturer has left. These models often have a suffix alongside the factory reference number and come with specially produced packaging. There are also a number of businesses and individuals producing one-off examples to a very high standard, such as the blue Sierra and white BMW produced in a fictitious Milton Football Club livery. Shown alongside these cars is an earlier Hornby-produced BMW for Printair (top left) and a Code 3 Mobil livery BMW for the Dutch SLN club (bottom right).

Weddings are expensive, and outside the church sits a McLaren decorated with glitter and €100 notes, which was used by participants in a 'Ladies' race at one of the Hornby/NSCC race weekends.

Scalextric has always had a good relationship with Lotus through the ages, producing many versions of their cars, and Lotus driver Jim Clark himself endorsed the brand in the two years before his fatal accident in the 1960s, appearing on the cover of catalogues Nos 6 and 7. The JPS livery used on many Lotus models can be seen here on two versions of the Lotus 77 that were produced in the 1970s. Hornby then went away from having cigarette advertising on their cars, as can be seen on the Lotus 98T (top of the picture) and the highly detailed Lotus 72 Team Classic Lotus made in the mid-2010s (back right) as part of a twin pack. However, the Lotus 72 was eventually released in full JPS livery again (leading car) but the packaging did carry warning notices advising 'not to be sold to children under 16'. A web search will usually turn up several sellers offering decals to get the correct livery on the car.

The picture shows Minis produced in the last decade. At first glance it seems there are two examples of the white and yellow Scalextric-sponsored car, but the one on the right is a high-detail solo release while that on the left is a super resistant car with blacked-out windows, as found in a set. Most cars in lower-priced sets are super resistant, like the blue and red cars, though some are also available as solo releases. Sometimes Scalextric have produced very similar cars for different sets with subtle changes in the colour scheme or tampo printing, giving the collector a vast array of cars to collect. This is particularly true of Mini, Lamborghini Gallardo, McLaren and Porsche models.

These Ferrari F40 football club-liveried cars were released as a set of seven in 1998. Due to licencing issues the box packaging says 'Premier Edition' rather than 'Premier League' on all the models, except for a small number of Chelsea cars that were released with Premier League packaging and are therefore now more expensive to buy than the others, even though the car inside is exactly the same. The cars came with a set of transfers to decorate the cars, and this was placed under the cardboard liner in the plastic box. Many owners are unaware of this, and when buying you should check that the sheet is still there if you want a mint boxed example. The club liveries that were released were Arsenal (red), Chelsea (blue), Liverpool (red), Newcastle United (black and white) and Tottenham Hotspur (white) from England, and Celtic (green) and Rangers (blue) from Scotland. The picture shows all seven liveries, without transfers applied, displayed in front of the board used to advertise this range at the time. Note that there are two Arsenal cars in the photograph: the one at the rear is a pre-production model that has JVC on the rear wing and the Arsenal badge on the roof positioned further back and the colour used on the 'A' logo and around the ARSENAL name is orange instead of red. There was a Manchester United version made but it was never released.

The Weird and Wonderful – Rare or Unusual Cars and Custom Scalextric

The most desirable car in the Scalextric range is probably the original 1960s Blue Type 59 Bugatti, which is shown earlier in the book (*see page 34*). It is estimated that there are just sixty to seventy left in existence, and even fewer of the Race Tuned version. Scalextric didn't release the car widely as it did not perform well, tending to overheat and melt.

The cream Bugatti shown here is a very interesting car as it was built by at the factory in Margate to test the old moulds and see if they could be used for a reissued version of the car. However, it was decided not to proceed with the project. The same process was also followed with the Auto Union with the same result, and that car is also pictured here.

In 1982 Scalextric made some Bugatti body tops in white, and a larger number of bases in black. When the cars were made up, the driver's arms and the mirrors were in black because they were on the same sprue as the base. The black bases were later used with a series of brightly coloured specially commissioned Bugattis, and later third parties completed remaining coloured cars fitted out with accessories in white metal or resin.

The proposed reissue of the vintage Bugatti around 1982 only got as far as testing the moulds and building up a few cars.

In this picture, the cream Type 59 Bugatti pre-non-production model races a green version that has been made up from resin, and which has all the correct steering, chrome accessories, maker's marks and model numbers on the base.

The top half of the Type 59 Bugatti, showing the black plastic that was used for the driver, mirrors, exhaust, radiator etc., which has been correctly melted into place by the factory. Many bodies were later built up by third parties using white metal or resin parts held in by glue.

On first looking at this picture it would seem to show the yellow 1960s C/71 Auto Union alongside the white C/91 race-tuned version. Note, however, that the white one has green wheels and the radiator is not chromed but is painted silver, as are the exhausts. The yellow car is an original, but the white one is the sister of the cream Bugatti as it is a mould test car made around 1980 with a view to reissue the Auto Union. Just as with the Bugatti, however, this never happened.

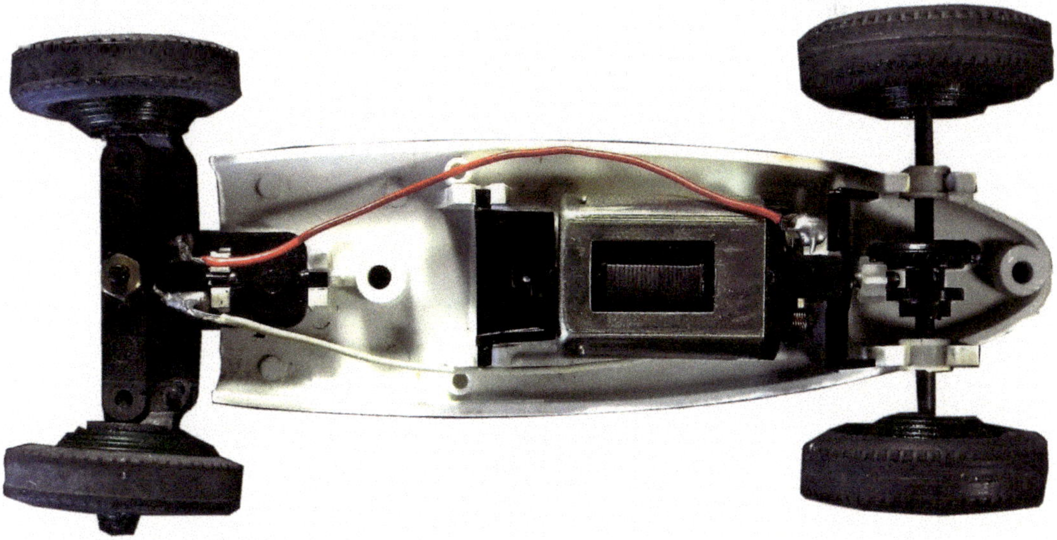

The inside of the 1980 pre-non-production Auto Union shows that it was fitted with a can motor but other than that it is the same as previous production models. The body colour, however, is slightly off white when compared with the C/91.

Left: One of the rarest of all – this Auto Union in a lovely deep blue is the only one in the world. It was made by one of the Minimodels employees and was supposed to be destroyed, as were all non-standard cars, but it survived with un-chromed accessories, so the radiator grille and exhausts are in their original clear condition, straight from the mould.

Below: Clear models have been produced over the years as one-off prototypes as well as limited runs of 100 cars for organisations. One such limited run car is the Lamborghini Diablo produced around the turn of this century in the 'Crystal Classics' series to promote a toy fair. The two BMWs also in the picture were probably prototype examples made in clear plastic. The one on the left also has a clear floor pan while the one on the right is in black.

Three Mercedes at the station. The brown and white car heading the group is a 250SL made in Spain, which was also listed in the UK catalogues. The 250SL at the rear is the open-top version in an unusual orange colour. Also made in Spain, it is quite rare. The white 190SL looks like a normal English-made car but is actually French, with a French box.

On first look, these are the twenty-first-century yellow and orange limited edition Mk 1 Ford Escorts, but they are actually beautifully resprayed and decaled 1970s Escorts.

And for comparison, here are the modern ones – the yellow one being a Scalextric Club car and the orange one a special limited edition of 1,500 cars.

These two hot rods have third party bodies mounted onto Scalextric chassis and running gear, courtesy of Glenn Mattioli.

A pair of customised Minis – the Clubman in gold metal-flake finish and the Metro in silver mirror finish – both courtesy of Glenn Mattioli.

The Porsche Spyder in this picture has been customised in the colours and number of the car driven by Stirling Moss in 1955. Here he encounters a Seat 600 on a mountain road in Europe. The Seat 600 in pale green is a fairly rare car, having been manufactured in Spain by the Exin company.

The car on the right is based on a Scalextric TR7 and is customised in matte black with an alien breaking through the bonnet lid and horns on the roof. The car next to it is a standard Hornby release – the *Mad Max 2* Ford XB Falcon in weathered matte black.

Two customised Scalextric Minis wait outside the church – an open-top Cooper and a purple metal-flake Clubman – courtesy of Glenn Mattioli.

The silver mirror finish Metro with a lime green Mini Cooper heading out of the woods.

On the right is the standard Scalextric Westwood Racing 1970s Mk 1 Ford Escort with working lights. On the left is a Mk 1 beast with supercharger, V8 pipes and rear aerofoil.

This Mk 1 Ford Escort, beautifully executed in silver, chases the gold Mini Clubman through the bridge.

Acknowledgements

The author would like to express greatest thanks to Steve Langford for supplying both his encyclopaedic knowledge and his cars in order for me to write the sections of the book on car livery variations and special editions.

Thanks also to Richard Johnson for his fine remodelling of some Scalextric cars to produce new classics in the true spirit of fun and enjoyment of this wonderful hobby.

I also thank both of the above for checking the text for me in the hope that we could remove as many mistakes as possible. While of course some will always slip through, I take full responsibility for those.

Thanks also to Meredith Hadfield and Bryony Mountfort for helping with the post-production photographic exploits, and both of them for delivering us the smoke and fire from the Spanish/American dragsters on the front cover.

Thank you very much to Jenny Burrell, who runs Bristol Slots, for letting me use her photographs of the rubber bridge embankments and Super124 driver figures. Thanks also for her general encouragement – always knowledgeable and fun to talk to.

Scenery provided by Derek Duncombe from Scale Model Studio makes this book come to life – I thank him for his contributions and urge anyone who likes his work to use his services for their own layout.

Finally, thank you to John Dunford for providing the locations for the outdoor shots taken in both sunshine and snow.

All photographs are by the author, except for those mentioned above.